The Complete Cooking Cookbook

Recipes for Everything You'll Want to Make

Marilyn D. Dubois

Earthenware. An ounce of dry lean cheese grated fine, and an equal quantity of quicklime mixed well together in three ounces of skim milk, will form a good cement for any articles of broken earthenware, when the rendering of the joint visible is reckoned of no consequence. A cement of the same nature may be made of quicklime tempered with the curd of milk, but the curd should either be made of whey or buttermilk. This cement, like the former, requires to be applied immediately after it is made, and it will effectually join any kind of earthenware or china.

EARWIGS. These insects are often destructive in gardens, especially where carnations, nuts, or filberts, pears and apples are reared. Their depredations on the flowers may be prevented by putting the bowl of a tobacco-pipe on the sticks which support them, into which they will creep in the day time, and may be destroyed. Green leaves of elder laid near fruit trees, or flower roots, will prevent their approach. Large quantities may be taken by placing short cuts of reed, bean or wheat straw, among the branches of fruit trees, and laying some on the ground near the root. Having committed their depredations in the night, they take refuge in these in the day time; the reed or straw may be taken away and burnt, and more put in its stead.—If unfortunately one of these disagreeable insects have crept into the ear, from their running so frequently about our garments, let the afflicted person lay his head upon a table, while some friend carefully drop into the ear a little sweet oil, or oil of almonds. A drop or two will be sufficient to destroy the insect, and remove the pain. An earwig may be extracted by applying a piece of apple to the ear, which will entice the insect to come out.

EDGEBONE OF BEEF. Skewer it up tight, and tie a broad fillet round it, to keep the skewers in their places. Put it in with plenty of cold water, and carefully catch the scum as it rises. When all the scum is removed, place the boiler on one side of the fire, to keep simmering slowly till it is done. A piece weighing ten pounds will take two hours, and larger in proportion. The slower it boils the better it will look, and the tenderer it will be: if allowed to boil quick at first, no art can make it tender afterwards. Dress plenty of carrots, as cold carrots are a general favourite with cold beef.

EEL BROTH. Clean half a pound of small eels, and set them on the fire with three pints of water, some parsley, a slice of onion, and a few peppercorns. Let them simmer till the eels are broken, and the broth good. Add salt, and strain it off. The above should make three half pints of broth, nourishing and good for weakly persons.

EEL PIE. Cut the eels in lengths of two or three inches, season with pepper and salt, and place them in a dish with some bits of butter, and a little water. Cover the dish with a paste, and bake it.

EEL SOUP. Put three pounds of small eels to two quarts of water, a crust of bread, three blades of mace, some whole pepper, an onion, and a bunch of sweet herbs. Cover them close, stew till the fish is quite broken, and then strain it off. Toast some bread, cut it into dice, and pour the soup on it boiling hot. Part of a carrot may be put in at first. This soup will be as rich as if made of meat. A quarter of a pint of rich cream, with a tea-spoonful of flour rubbed smooth in it, is a great improvement.

EGGS. In new-laid eggs there is a small division of the skin at the end of the shell, which is filled with air, and is perceptible to the eye. On looking through them against the sun or a candle, they will be tolerably clear; but if they shake in the shell, they are not fresh. Another way to distinguish fresh eggs, is to put the large end to the tongue; if it feels warm, it is new and good. Eggs may be bought cheapest in the spring, when the hens first begin to lay, before they set: in Lent and at Easter they become dear. They may be preserved fresh for some time by dipping them in boiling water, and instantly taking them out, or by oiling the shell, either of which will prevent the air from passing through. They may also be kept on shelves with small holes to receive one in each, and be turned every other day; or close packed in a keg, and covered with strong lime water. A still better way of preserving eggs in a fresh state is to dip them in a solution of gum-arabic in water, and then imbed them in powdered charcoal. The gum-arabic answers the purpose of a varnish for the eggs, much better than any resinous gum, as it can easily be removed by washing them in water, and is a much cheaper preparation than any other. If eggs are greased the oily matter becomes rancid, and infallibly hastens the putrefaction of the eggs. But being varnished with gum water, and imbedded in charcoal, they will keep for many years, and may be removed from one climate to another.

EGGS AND BACON. Lay some slices of fine streaked bacon in a clean dish, and toast them before the fire in a cheese-toaster, turning them when the upper side is browned; or if it be wished to have them mellow and soft, rather than curled and crisp, parboil the slices before they are toasted and do them lightly. Clear dripping or lard is to be preferred to butter for frying the eggs, and be sure that the fryingpan is quite clean before it is put in. When the fat is hot, break two or three eggs into it. Do not turn them; but while they are frying, keep pouring some of the fat over them with a spoon. When the yolk just begins to look white, which it will in about two minutes, they are enough, and the white must not be suffered to lose its transparency. Take up the eggs with a tin slice, drain the fat from them, trim them neatly, and send them up with the bacon round them.

EGGS AND ONIONS. Boil some eggs hard, take out the yolks whole, and cut the whites in slices. Fry some onions and mushrooms, put in the whites, and keep them turning. Pour off the fat, flour the onions, and add a little gravy. Boil them up, then put in the yolks, with a little pepper and salt. Simmer the whole about a minute, and serve it up.

EGGS FOR SALLAD. Boil a couple of eggs for twelve minutes, and put them into a bason of cold water, to render the yolks firm and hard. Rub them through a sieve with a wooden spoon, and mix them with a spoonful of water, or fine double cream, and add two table-spoonfuls of oil or melted butter. When these are well mixed, add by degrees a tea-spoonful of salt, or powdered lump sugar, and the same of made mustard. Add very gradually three table-spoonfuls of vinegar, rub it with the other ingredients till thoroughly incorporated, and cut up the white of the egg to garnish the top of the sallad. Let the sauce remain at the bottom of the bowl, and do not stir up the sallad till it is to be eaten. This sauce is equally good with cold meat, cold fish, or for cucumbers, celery, and radishes.

EGGS FOR THE SICK. Eggs very little boiled or poached, when taken in small quantities, convey much nourishment. The yolk only, when dressed, should be eaten by invalids. An egg divided, and the yolk and white beaten separately, then mixed with a glass of wine, will afford two very wholesome draughts, and prove lighter than when taken together. An egg broken into a cup of tea, or beaten and mixed with a bason of milk, makes a breakfast more supporting than tea only.

EGGS FOR TURTLE. Beat in a mortar three yolks of eggs that have been boiled hard. Make it into a paste with the yolk of a raw one, roll it into small balls, and throw them into boiling water for two minutes to harden.

EGG BALLS. Boil the eggs hard, and put them in cold water. Take out the yolks, and pound them fine in a mortar, wetting them with raw yolks, about one to three. Season them with salt and white pepper, dry them with flour, and roll them into small balls, as they swell very much in boiling. When dressed, boil them in gravy for a minute.

EGG PIE. Boil twelve eggs hard, and chop them with one pound of marrow, or beef suet. Season with a little cinnamon and nutmeg finely beaten, adding one pound of currants clean washed and picked, two or three spoonfuls of cream, a little sweet wine, and rose water. Mix all together, and fill the pie: when it is baked, stir in half a pound of fresh butter, and the juice of a lemon.

EGG MINCE PIES. Boil six eggs hard, shred them small, and double the quantity of shred suet. Then add a pound of currants washed and picked, or more if the eggs were large; the peel of one lemon shred very fine, and the juice; six spoonfuls of sweet wine, mace, nutmeg, sugar, a very little salt; orange, lemon, and citron, candied. Cover the pies with a light paste.

EGG SAUCE. Boil the eggs hard, chop them fine, and put them into melted butter. If thrown into cold water after being boiled, the yolks will become firmer, will be easier to cut, and the surface be prevented from turning black. Egg sauce will be found an agreeable accompaniment to roast fowl, or salt fish.

EGG WINE. Beat up an egg, and mix it with a spoonful of cold water. Set on the fire a glass of white wine, half a glass of water, with sugar and nutmeg. When it boils, pour a little of it to the egg by degrees, till the whole is mixed, and stir it well. Then return the whole into the saucepan, put it on a gentle fire, stir it one way for about a minute. If it boil, or the egg be stale, it will curdle. The wine may be made without warming the egg; it is then lighter on the stomach, though not so pleasant to the taste. Serve it with toast.

ELDER. The fœtid smell of the common elder is such, especially of the dwarf elder, that if the leaves and branches be strewed among cabbage and cauliflower plants, or turnips, it will secure them from the ravages of flies and caterpillars; and if hung on the branches of trees, it will protect them from the effects of blight. Or if put into the subterraneous paths of the moles, it will drive them from the garden. An infusion of the leaves in water, and sprinkled over rose-buds and other flowers, will preserve them from the depredations of the caterpillar.

ELDER ROB. Clear some ripe elder-berries from the stalks, bake them in covered jars for two hours, and squeeze the juice through a strainer. To four quarts of juice put one pound of sugar, and stir it over the fire till reduced to one quart. When cold, tie it down with a bladder, and keep it in a dry place. It is very good for sore throats and fevers.

ELDER SYRUP. Pick off the elder berries when fully ripe, bake them in a stone jar, strain them through a coarse sieve, and put the juice into a clean kettle. To every quart of juice add a pound of fine soft sugar, boil and skim it well: when it is clear, pour it into a jar, cool it, and cover it down. Half a pint of this syrup added to a gallon of new made wine, will give it a very rich flavour, or it may be used for other purposes.

ELDER WINE. Pick the berries from the stalk, and to every quart allow two quarts of water. Boil them half an hour, run the liquor and break the fruit through a hair sieve, and to every quart of juice put three quarters of a pound of moist sugar. Boil the whole a quarter of an hour, with some peppercorns, ginger, and a few cloves. Pour it into a tub, and when of a proper warmth, into the barrel, with toast and yeast to work, which there is more difficulty to make it do than most other liquors. When it ceases to hiss, put a quart of brandy to eight gallons, and stop it up. Bottle it in the spring, or at Christmas.—To make white elder wine, very much like Frontiniac, boil eighteen pounds of white powder sugar with six gallons of water, and two whites of eggs well beaten. Skim it clean, and but in a quarter of a peck of elder flowers from the tree that bears white berries, but do not keep them on the fire. Stir it when nearly cold, and but in six spoonfuls of lemon juice, four or five spoonfuls of yeast, and beat it well into the liquor. Stir it every day, put into the cask six pounds of the best raisins stoned, and tun the wine. Stop it close, and bottle it in six months. When well kept, this wine will pass for Frontiniac.

ELDER FLOWER WINE. To six gallons of spring water put six pounds of sun raisins cut small, and a dozen pounds of fine sugar: boil the whole together for about an hour and a half. When the liquor is cold, put in half a peck of ripe elder flowers, with about a gill of lemon juice, and half the quantity of ale yeast. Cover it up, and after standing three days, strain it off. Pour it into a cask that is quite clean, and that will hold it with ease. When this is done, add a quart of Rhenish wine to every gallon of liquor, and let the bung be lightly put in for twelve or fourteen days. Then stop it down fast, and put it in a cool dry place for four or five months, till it is quite settled and fine: then bottle it off.

ENGLISH BAMBOO. About the middle of May, cut some large young shoots of elder; strip off the outward peel, and soak them all night in some strong salt and water. Dry them separately in a cloth, and have in readiness the following pickle. To a quart of vinegar put an ounce of white pepper, an ounce of sliced ginger, a little mace and pimento, all boiled together. Put the elder shoots into a stone jar, pour on the liquor boiling hot, stop it up close, and set it by the fire two hours, turning the jar often to keep it hot. If not green when cold, strain off the liquor, pour it on boiling again, and keep it hot as before.—Or if it be intended to make Indian pickle, the addition of these shoots will be found to be a great improvement. In this case it will only be necessary to pour boiling vinegar and mustard seed on them, and to keep them till the jar of pickles shall be ready to receive them. The cluster of elder flowers before it opens, makes a delicious pickle to eat with boiled mutton. It is prepared by only pouring vinegar over the flowers.

ENGLISH BRANDY. English or British brandy may be made in smaller quantities, according to the following proportions. To sixty gallons of clear rectified spirits, put one pound of sweet spirit of nitre, one pound of cassia buds ground, one pound of bitter almond meal, (the cassia and almond meal to be mixed together before they are put to the spirits) two ounces of sliced orris root, and about thirty or forty prune stones pounded. Shake the whole well together, two or three times a day, for three days or more. Let them settle, then pour in one gallon of the best wine vinegar; and add to every four gallons, one gallon of foreign brandy.

ENGLISH CHAMPAIGNE. Take gooseberries before they are ripe, crush them with a mallet in a wooden bowl; and to every gallon of fruit, put a gallon of water. Let it stand two days, stirring it well. Squeeze the mixture with the hands through a hop sieve, then measure the liquor, and to every gallon put three pounds and a half of loaf sugar. Mix it well in the tub, and let it stand one day. Put a bottle of the best brandy into the cask, which leave open five or six weeks, taking off the scum as it rises. Then stop it up, and let it stand one year in the barrel before it is bottled.

ENGLISH SHERRY. Boil thirty pounds of lump sugar in ten gallons of water, and clear it of the scum. When cold, put a quart of new alewort to every gallon of liquor, and let it work in the tub a day or two. Then put it into a cask with a pound of sugar candy, six pounds of fine raisins, a pint of brandy, and two ounces of isinglass. When the fermentation is over, stop it close: let it stand eight months, rack it off, and add a little more brandy. Return it to the cask again, and let it stand four months before it is bottled.

ENGLISH WINES. During the high price of foreign wine, home-made wines will be found particularly useful; and though sugar is dear, they may be prepared at a quarter of the expence. If carefully made, and kept three or four years, a proportionable strength being given, they would answer the purpose of foreign wines for health, and cause a very considerable reduction in the expenditure. Sugar and water are the principal basis of home-made wine; and when these require to be boiled, it is proper to beat up the whites of eggs to a froth, and mix them with the water when cold, in the proportion of one egg to a gallon. When the sugar and water are boiled, the liquor should be cooled quickly; and if not for wines that require fermenting, it may be put into the cask when cold. If the wine is to be fermented, the yeast should be put into it when it is milk-warm; but must not be left more than two nights to ferment, before it is put into the cask. Particular care should be taken to have the cask sweet and dry, and washed inside with a little brandy, before the wine is tunned, but it should not be bunged up close till it has done fermenting. After standing three or four months, it will be necessary to taste the wine, to know whether it be fit to draw off. If not sweet enough, some sugar should be added, or draw it off into another cask, and put in some sugar-candy: but if too sweet, let it stand a little longer. When the wine is racked, the dregs may be drained through a flannel bag; and the wine, if not clear enough for the table, may be used for sauce.

ESSENCE OF ALLSPICE. Take a dram of the oil of pimento, and mix it by degrees with two ounces of strong spirit of wine. A few drops will give the flavour of allspice to a pint of gravy, or mulled wine.

ESSENCE OF ANCHOVY. Put into a marble mortar ten or twelve fine mellow anchovies, that have been well pickled, and pound them to a pulp. Put this into a clean well-tinned saucepan, then put a table-spoonful of cold water into the mortar, shake it round, and pour it to the pounded anchovies. Set them by the side of a slow fire, frequently stirring them together till they are melted, which they will be in the course of five minutes. Now stir in a quarter of a dram of good cayenne, and let it remain by the fire a few minutes longer. Rub it through a hair sieve with the back of a wooden spoon, and keep it stopped very closely: if the air gets to it, it is spoiled directly. Essence of anchovy is made sometimes with sherry, or madeira, instead of water, or with the addition of mushroom ketchup.

ESSENCE OF CAYENNE. Put half an ounce of cayenne pepper into half a pint of wine or brandy, let it steep a fortnight, and then pour off the clear liquor. This article is very convenient for the extempore seasoning and finishing of soups and sauces, its flavour being instantly and equally diffused.

ESSENCE OF CELERY. Steep in a quarter of a pint of brandy, or proof spirit, half an ounce of celery seed bruised, and let it stand a fortnight. A few drops will immediately flavour a pint of broth, and are an excellent addition to pease, and other soups.

ESSENCE OF CLOVES. Mix together two ounces of the strongest spirit of wine, and a dram of the oil of cloves. Nutmeg, cinnamon, and mace are prepared in the same manner.

ESSENCE OF FLOWERS. Select a quantity of the petals of any flowers which have an agreeable fragrance, lay them in an earthen vessel, and sprinkle a little fine salt upon them. Then dip some cotton into the best Florence oil, and lay it thin upon the flowers; continue a layer of petals, and a layer of cotton, till the vessel is full. It is then to be closed down with a bladder, and exposed to the heat of the sun. In about a fortnight a fragrant oil may be squeezed away from the whole mass, which will yield a rich perfume.

ESSENCE OF GINGER. Grate three ounces of ginger, and an ounce of thin lemon peel, into a quart of brandy, or proof spirit, and let it stand for ten days, shaking it up each day. If ginger is taken to produce an immediate effect, to warm the stomach, or dispel flatulence, this will be found the best preparation.

ESSENCE OF LAVENDER. Take the blossoms from the stalks in warm weather, and spread them in the shade for twenty-four hours on a linen cloth; then bruise and put them into warm water, and leave them closely covered in a still for four or five hours near the fire. After this the blossoms may be distilled in the usual way.

ESSENCE OF LEMON PEEL. Wash and brush clean the lemons, and let them get perfectly dry. Take a lump of fine sugar, and rub them till all the yellow rind is taken up by the sugar; scrape off the surface of the sugar into a preserving pot, and press it hard down. Cover it very close, and it will keep for some time. By this process is obtained the whole of the fine essential oil, which contains the flavour.

ESSENCE OF MUSHROOMS. This delicate relish is made by sprinkling a little salt over some mushrooms, and mashing them three hours after. Next day strain off the liquor, put it into a stewpan, and boil it till reduced one half. It will not keep long, but is preferable to any of the ketchups. An artificial bed of mushrooms would supply this article all the year round.

ESSENCE OF OYSTERS. Take fine fresh Milton oysters, wash them in their own liquor, skim it, and pound them in a marble mortar. To a pint of oysters add a pint of sherry, boil them up, and add an ounce of salt, two drams of pounded mace, and one of cayenne. Let it just boil up again, skim it, and rub it through a sieve. When cold, bottle and cork it well, and seal it down. This composition very agreeably heightens the flavour of white sauces, and white made-dishes. If a glass of brandy be added to the essence, it will keep a considerable time longer than oysters are out of season.

ESSENCE OF SHALOT. Peel, mince, and pound in a mortar, three ounces of shalots, and infuse them in a pint of sherry for three days. Then pour off the clear liquor on three ounces more of shalots, and let the wine remain on them ten days longer. An ounce of scraped horseradish may be added to the above, and a little thin lemon peel. This will impart a fine flavour to soups, sauces, hashes, and various other dishes.

ESSENCE OF SOAP. For washing or shaving, the essence of soap is very superior to what is commonly used for these purposes, and a very small quantity will make an excellent lather. Mix two ounces of salt of tartar with half a pound of soap finely sliced, put them into a quart of spirits of wine, in a bottle that will contain twice the quantity. Tie it down with a bladder, prick a pin through it for the air to escape, set it to digest in a gentle heat, and shake up the contents. When the soap is dissolved, filter the liquor through some paper to free it from impurities, and scent it with burgamot or essence of lemon.

ESSENCE OF TURTLE. Mix together one wine-glassful of the essence of anchovy, one and a half of shalot wine, four wine-glassfuls of Basil wine, two ditto of mushroom ketchup, one dram of lemon acid, three quarters of an ounce of lemon peel very thinly pared, and a quarter of an ounce of curry powder, and let them steep together for a week. The essence thus obtained will be found convenient to flavour soup, sauce, potted meats, savoury patties, and various other articles.

EVACUATIONS. Few things are more conducive to health than keeping the body regular, and paying attention to the common evacuations. A proper medium between costiveness and laxness is highly desirable, and can only be obtained by regularity in diet, sleep, and exercise. Irregularity in eating and drinking disturbs every part of the animal economy, and never fails to produce diseases. Too much or too little food will have this effect: the former generally occasions looseness, and the latter costiveness; and both have a tendency to injure health. Persons who have frequent recourse to medicine for preventing costiveness, seldom fail to ruin their constitution. They ought rather to remove the evil by diet than by drugs, by avoiding every thing of a hot or binding nature, by going thinly clothed, walking in the open air, and acquiring the habit of a regular discharge by a stated visit to the place of retreat. Habitual looseness is often owing to an obstructed perspiration: persons thus afflicted should keep their feet warm, and wear flannel next the skin. Their diet also should be of an astringent quality, and such as tends to strengthen the bowels. For this purpose, fine bread, cheese, eggs, rice milk, red wine, or brandy and water would be proper.—Insensible perspiration is one of the principal discharges from the human body, and is of such importance to health, that few diseases attack us while it goes on properly; but when obstructed, the whole frame is soon disordered, and danger meets us in every form. The common cause of obstructed perspiration, or taking cold, is the sudden changes of the weather; and the best means of fortifying the body is to be abroad every day, and breathe freely in the open air. Much danger arises from wet feet and wet clothes, and persons who are much abroad are exposed to these things. The best way is to change wet clothes as soon as possible, or to keep in motion till they be dry, but by no means to sit or lie down. Early habits may indeed inure people to wet clothes and wet feet without any danger, but persons of a delicate constitution cannot be too careful. Perspiration is often obstructed by other means, but it is in all cases attended with considerable danger. Sudden transitions from heat to cold, drinking freely of cold water after being heated with violent exercise, sitting near an open window when the room is hot, plunging into cold water in a state of perspiration, or going into the cold air immediately after sitting in a warm room, are among the various means by which the health of thousands is constantly ruined; and more die of colds than are killed by plagues, or slain in battle.

EVE'S PUDDING. Grate three quarters of a pound of bread; mix it with the same quantity of shred suet, the same of apples, and also of currants. Mix with these the whole of four eggs, and the rind of half a lemon shred fine. Put it into a shape, and boil it three hours. Serve with pudding sauce, the juice of half a lemon, and a little nutmeg.

EXERCISE. Whether man were originally intended for labour or not, it is evident from the human structure, that exercise is not less necessary than food, for the preservation of health. It is generally seen among the labouring part of the community, that industry places them above want, and activity serves them instead of physic. It seems to be the established law of the animal creation, that without exercise no creature should enjoy health, or be able to find subsistence. Every creature, except man, takes as much of it as is necessary: he alone deviates from this original law, and suffers accordingly. Weak nerves, and glandular obstructions, which are now so common, are the constant companions of inactivity. We seldom hear the active or laborious complain of nervous diseases: indeed many have been cured of them by being reduced to the necessity of labouring for their own support. This shews the source from which such disorders flow, and the means by which they may be prevented. It is evident that health cannot be enjoyed where the perspiration is not duly carried on; but that can never be the case where exercise is neglected. Hence it is that the inactive are continually complaining of pains of the stomach, flatulencies, and various other disorders which cannot be removed by medicine, but might be effectually cured by a course of vigorous exercise. But to render this in the highest degree beneficial, it should always be taken in the open air, especially in the morning, while the stomach is empty, and the body refreshed with sleep. The morning air braces and strengthens the nerves, and in some measure answers the purpose of a cold bath. Every thing that induces people to sit still, except it be some necessary employment, ought to be avoided; and if exercise cannot be had in the open air, it should be attended to as far as possible within doors. Violent exertions however are no more to be recommended than inactivity; for whatever fatigues the body, prevents the benefit of exercise, and tends to weaken rather than strengthen it. Fast walking, immediately before or after meals, is highly pernicious, and necessarily accelerates the circulation of the blood, which is attended with imminent danger to the head or brain. On the other hand, indolence not only occasions diseases, and renders men useless to society, but it is the parent of vice. The mind, if not engaged in some useful pursuit, is constantly in search of ideal pleasures, or impressed with the apprehension of some imaginary evil; and from these sources proceed most of the miseries of mankind. An active life is the best guardian of virtue, and the greatest preservative of health.

F.

FACSIMILES. To produce a facsimile of any writing, the pen should be made of glass enamel, the point being small and finely polished, so that the part above the point may be large enough to hold as much or more ink than a common writing pen. A mixture of equal parts of Frankfort black, and fresh butter, is now to be smeared over sheets of paper, and is to be rubbed off after a certain time. The paper thus smeared is to be pressed for some hours, taking care to have sheets of blotting paper between each of the sheets of black paper. When fit for use, writing paper is put between sheets of blackened paper, and the upper sheet is to be written on, with common ink, by the glass or enamel pen. By this method, not only the copy is obtained on which the pen writes, but also two or more, made by means of the blackened paper.

FAMILY PIES. To make a plain trust for pies to be eaten hot, or for fruit puddings, cut some thin slices of beef suet, lay them in some flour, mix it with cold water, and roll it till it is quite soft. Or make a paste of half a pound of butter or lard, and a pound and a half of flour. Mix it with water, work it up, roll it out twice, and cover the dish with it.

FAMILY WINE. An excellent compound wine, suited to family use, may be made of equal parts of red, white, and black currants, ripe cherries and raspberries, well bruised, and mixed with soft water, in the proportion of four pounds of fruit to one gallon of water. When strained and pressed, three pounds of moist sugar are to be added to each gallon of liquid. After standing open for three days, during which it is to be stirred frequently, it is to be put into a barrel, and left for a fortnight to work, when a ninth part of brandy is to be added, and the whole bunged down. In a few months it will be a most excellent wine.

FATTING FOWLS. Chickens or fowls may be fatted in four or five days, by setting some rice over the fire with skimmed milk, as much as will serve for one day. Let it boil till the rice is quite swelled, and add a tea-spoonful of sugar. Feed them three times a day, in common pans, giving them only as much as will quite fill them at once. Before they are fed again, set the pans in water, that no sourness may be conveyed to the fowls, as that would prevent their fattening. Let them drink clean water, or the milk of the rice; but when rice is given them, after being perfectly soaked, let as much of the moisture as possible be drawn from it. By this method the flesh will have a clean whiteness, which no other food gives; and when it is considered how far a pound of rice will go, and how much time is saved by this mode, it will be found nearly as cheap as any other food, especially if it is to be purchased. The chicken pen should be cleaned every day, and no food given for sixteen hours before poultry is to be killed.

FAWN. A fawn, like a sucking pig, should be dressed almost as soon as it is killed. When very young, it is trussed, stuffed, and spitted the same as a hare. But they are better eating when of the size of a house lamb, and then roasted in quarters: the hind quarter is most esteemed. The meat must be put down to a very quick fire, and either basted all the time it is roasting, or be covered with sheets of fat bacon. When done, baste it with butter, and dredge it with a little salt and flour, till a nice froth is set upon it. Serve it up with venison sauce. If a fawn be half roasted as soon as received, and afterwards made into a hash, it will be very fine.

FEAR. Sudden fear, or an unexpected fright, often produces epileptic fits, and other dangerous disorders. Many young people have lost their lives or their senses by the foolish attempts of producing violent alarm, and the mind has been thrown into such disorders as never again to act with regularity. A settled dread and anxiety not only dispose the body to diseases, but often render those diseases fatal, which a cheerful mind would overcome; and the constant dread of some future evil, has been known to bring on the very evil itself. A mild and sympathizing behaviour towards the afflicted will do them more good than medicine, and he is the best physician and the best friend who administers the consolation of hope.

FEATHERS. Where poultry is usually sold ready picked, the feathers which occasionally come in small quantities are neglected; but care should be taken to put them into a clean tub, and as they dry to change them into paper bags, in small quantities. They should hang in a dry kitchen to season; fresh ones must not be added to those in part dried, or they will occasion a musty smell, but they should go through the same process. In a few months they will be fit to add to beds, or to make pillows, without the usual mode of drying them in a cool oven, which may be pursued if they are wanted before five or six months.

FEATHERS CLEANED. In order to clear feathers from animal oil, dissolve a pound of quick lime in a gallon of clear water; and pour off the clear lime-water for use, at the time it is wanted. Put the feathers to be cleaned in a tub, and add to them a sufficient quantity of the clear lime-water, so as to cover them about three inches. The feathers, when thoroughly moistened, will sink down, and should remain in the lime-water for three or four days; after which, the foul liquor should be separated from them by laying them on a sieve. They are afterwards to be washed in clean water, and dried on nets, the meshes being about the same fineness as those of cabbage nets. They must be shaken from time to time on the nets; as they dry, they will fall through the meshes, and are to be collected for use. The admission of air will be serviceable in the drying, and the whole process may be completed in about three weeks. The feathers, after being thus prepared, want nothing farther than beating, to be used either for beds, bolsters, pillows, or cushions.

FEET. To prevent corns from growing on the feet, wear easy shoes, and bathe the feet often in lukewarm water, with a little salt and potash dissolved in it. The corn itself may be completely destroyed by rubbing it daily with a little caustic solution of potash, till a soft and flexible skin is formed. For chilblains, soak the feet in warm bran and water and rub them well with flour of mustard. This should be done before the chilblains begin to break.

FENNEL SAUCE. Boil fennel and parsley, tied together in a bunch; chop it small, and stir it up with melted butter. This sauce is generally eaten with mackarel.

FEVER DRINK. To make a refreshing drink in a fever, put into a stone jug a little tea sage, two sprigs of balm, and a small quantity of wood sorrel, having first washed and dried them. Peel thin a small lemon, and clear from the white; slice it, and put in a bit of the peel. Then pour in three pints of boiling water, sweeten, and cover it close.—Another drink. Wash extremely well an ounce of pearl barley; shift it twice, then put to it three pints of water, an ounce of sweet almonds beaten fine, and a bit of lemon peel. Boil the liquor smooth, put in a little syrup of lemons, and capillaire.—Another way is to boil three pints of water with an ounce and a half of tamarinds, three ounces of currants, and two ounces of stoned raisins, till nearly a third is consumed. Strain it on a bit of lemon peel, which should be removed in the course of an hour, or it will infuse a bitter taste.

FILLET OF VEAL. Stuff it well under the udder, at the bone, and quite through to the shank. Put it into the oven, with a pint of water under it, till it comes to a fine brown. Then put it in a stewpan with three pints of gravy, and stew it quite tender. Add a tea-spoonful of lemon pickle, a large spoonful of browning, one of ketchup, and a little cayenne; thicken it with a bit of butter rolled in flour. Put the veal in a dish, strain the gravy over it, and lay round it forcemeat balls. Garnish with pickle and lemon.

FINE CAKE. To make an excellent cake, rub two pounds of fine dry flour with one of butter, washed in plain and then in rose water. Mix with it three spoonfuls of yeast, in a little warm milk and water. Set it to rise an hour and a half before the fire, and then beat into it two pounds of currants, carefully washed and picked, and one pound of sifted sugar. Add four ounces of almonds, six ounces of stoned raisins chopped fine, half a nutmeg, cinnamon, allspice, and a few cloves, the peel of a lemon shred very fine, a glass of wine, one of brandy, twelve yolks and whites of eggs beat separately, with orange, citron, and lemon. Beat them up well together, butter the pan, and bake in a quick oven.—To make a still finer cake, wash two pounds and a half of fresh butter in water first, and then in rose water, and beat the butter to a cream. Beat up twenty eggs, yolks and whites, separately, half an hour each. Have ready two pounds and a half of the finest flour well dried and kept hot, likewise a pound and a half of loaf sugar pounded and sifted, an ounce of spice in very fine powder, three pounds of currants nicely cleaned and dry, half a pound of almonds blanched, and three quarters of a pound of sweetmeats cut small. Let all be kept by the fire, and mix the dry ingredients. Pour the eggs strained to the butter, mix half a glass of sweet wine with a full glass of brandy, and pour it to the butter and eggs, mixing them well together. Add the dry ingredients by degrees, and beat them together thoroughly for a great length of time. Having prepared and stoned half a pound of jar raisins, chopped as fine as possible, mix them carefully, so that there shall be no lumps, and add a teacupful of orange flower water. Beat the ingredients together a full hour at least. Have a hoop well buttered, or a tin or copper cake-pan; take a white paper, doubled and buttered, and put in the pan round the edge, if the cake batter fill it more than three parts, for space should be allowed for rising. Bake it in a quick oven: three hours will be requisite.

FINE CRUST. For orange cheesecakes, or sweetmeats, when intended to be particularly nice, the following fine crust may be prepared. Dry a pound of the finest flour and mix with it three ounces of refined sugar. Work up half a pound of butter with the hand till it comes to a froth, put the flour into it by degrees, adding the yolks of three and the whites of two eggs, well beaten and strained. If too thin, add a little flour and sugar to make it fit to roll. Line some pattipans, and fill them: a little more than fifteen minutes will bake them. Beat up some refined sugar with the white of an egg, as thick as possible, and ice the articles all over as soon as they are baked. Then return them to the oven to harden, and serve them up cold, with fresh butter. Salt butter will make a very fine flaky crust, but if for mince pies, or any sweet things, it should first be washed.

FIRE ARMS. The danger of improperly loading fire arms chiefly arises from not ramming the wadding close to the powder; and then when a fowling-piece is discharged, it is very likely to burst in pieces. This circumstance, though well known, is often neglected, and various accidents are occasioned by it. Hence when a screw barrel pistol is to be loaded, care should be taken that the cavity for the powder be entirely filled with it, so as to leave no space between the powder and the ball. For the same reason, if the bottom of a large tree is to be shivered with gunpowder, a space must be left between the charge and the wadding, and the powder will tear it asunder. But considering the numerous accidents that are constantly occurring, from the incautious use of fire arms, the utmost care should be taken not to place them within the reach of children or of servants, and in no instance to lay them up without previously drawing the charge.

FIRE IRONS. To preserve them from rust, when not in use, they should be wrapped up in baize, and kept in a dry place. Or to preserve them more effectually, let them be smeared over with fresh mutton suet, and dusted with unslaked lime, pounded and tied up in muslin. Irons so prepared will keep many months. Use no oil for them at any time, except a little salad oil, there being water in all other, which would soon produce rust.

FIRMITY. To make Somersetshire firmity, boil a quart of fine wheat, and add by degrees two quarts of new milk. Pick and wash four ounces of currants, stir them in the jelly, and boil them together till all is done. Beat the yolks of three eggs, and a little nutmeg, with two or three spoonfuls of milk, and add to the boiling. Sweeten the whole, and serve it in a deep dish, either warm or cold.

FISH. In dressing fish of any kind for the table, great care is necessary in cleaning it. It is a common error to wash it too much, and by this means the flavour is diminished. If the fish is to be boiled, after it is cleaned, a little salt and vinegar should be put into the water, to give it firmness. Codfish, whiting, and haddock, are far better if a little salted, and kept a day; and if the weather be not very hot, they will be good two days. When fish is cheap and plentiful, and a larger quantity is purchased than is immediately wanted, it would be proper to pot or pickle such as will bear it, or salt and hang it up, or fry it a little, that it may serve for stewing the next day. Fresh water fish having frequently a muddy smell and taste, should be soaked in strong salt and water, after it has been well cleaned. If of a sufficient size, it may be scalded in salt and water, and afterwards dried and dressed. Fish should be put into cold water, and set on the fire to do very gently, or the outside will break before the inner part is done. Crimp fish is to be put into boiling water; and when it boils up, pour in a little cold water to check extreme heat, and simmer it a few minutes. The fish plate on which it is done, may be drawn up, to see if it be ready, which may be known by its easily separating from the bone. It should then be immediately taken out of the water, or it will become woolly. The fish plate should be set crossways over the kettle, to keep hot for serving; and a clean cloth over the fish, to prevent its losing its colour. Small fish nicely fried, covered with egg and crumbs, make a dish far more elegant than if served plain. Great attention is required in garnishing fish, by using plenty of horseradish, parsley, and lemon. When well done, and with very good sauce, fish is more attended to than almost any other dish. The liver and roe should be placed on the dish in order that they may be distributed in the course of serving.—If fish is to be fried or broiled, it must be dried in a nice soft cloth, after it is well cleaned and washed. If for frying, smear it over with egg, and sprinkle on it some fine crumbs of bread. If done a second time with the egg and bread, the fish will look so much the better. Put on the fire a stout fryingpan, with a large quantity of lard or dripping boiling hot, plunge the fish into it, and let it fry tolerably quick, till the colour is of a fine brown yellow. If it be done enough before it has obtained a proper degree of colour, the pan must be drawn to the side of the fire. Take it up carefully, and either place it on a large sieve turned upwards, and to be kept for that purpose only, or on the under side of a dish to drain. If required to be very nice, a sheet of writing paper must be placed to receive the fish, that it may be free from all grease; it must also be of a beautiful colour, and all the crumbs appear distinct. The same dripping, adding a little that is fresh, will serve a second time. Butter gives a bad colour, oil is the best, if the expense be no objection. Garnish with a fringe of fresh curled parsley. If fried parsley be used, it must be washed and picked, and thrown into fresh water; when the lard or dripping boils, throw the parsley into it immediately from the water, and instantly it will be green and crisp, and must be taken up with a slice.—If fish is to be broiled, it must be seasoned, floured, and laid on a very clean gridiron, which when hot, should be rubbed with a bit of suet, to prevent the fish from sticking. It must be broiled over a very clear fire, that it may not taste smoky; and not too near, that it may not be scorched.

FISH GRAVY. Skin two or three eels, or some flounders; gut and wash them very clean, cut them into small pieces, and put them into a saucepan. Cover them with water, and add a little crust of toasted bread, two blades of mace, some whole pepper, sweet herbs, a piece of lemon peel, an anchovy or two, and a tea-spoonful of horse-radish. Cover the saucepan close, and let it simmer; then add a little butter and flour, and boil with the above.

FISH PIE. To make a fine fish pie, boil two pounds of small eels. Cut the fins quite close, pick off the flesh, and return the bones into the liquor, with a little mace, pepper, salt, and a slice of onion. Then boil it till it is quite rich, and strain it. Make forcemeat of the flesh, with an anchovy, a little parsley, lemon peel, salt, pepper, and crumbs, and four ounces of butter warmed. Lay it at the bottom of the dish: then take the flesh of soles, small cod, or dressed turbot, and rub it with salt and pepper. Lay this on the forcemeat, pour on the gravy, and bake it. If cod or soles are used, the skin and fins must be taken off.

FISH SAUCE. Put into a very nice tin saucepan a pint of port wine, a gill of mountain, half a pint of fine walnut ketchup, twelve anchovies with the liquor that belongs to them, a gill of walnut pickle, the rind and juice of a large lemon, four or five shalots, a flavour of cayenne, three ounces of scraped horse-radish, three blades of mace, and two tea-spoonfuls of made mustard. Boil it all gently, till the rawness goes off, and put it into small bottles for use. Cork them very close and seal the top.—Or chop two dozen of anchovies not washed, and ten shalots, and scrape three spoonfuls of horseradish. Then add ten blades of mace, twelve cloves, two sliced lemons, half a pint of anchovy liquor, a quart of hock or Rhenish wine, and a pint of water. Boil it down to a quart, and strain it off. When cold, add three large spoonfuls of walnut ketchup, and put the sauce into small bottles well corked.—To make fish sauce without butter, simmer very gently a quarter of a pint of vinegar, and half a pint of soft water, with an onion. Add four cloves, and two blades of mace, slightly bruised, and half a tea-spoonful of black pepper. When the onion is quite tender, chop it small with two anchovies, and set the whole on the fire to boil for a few minutes, with a spoonful of ketchup. Prepare in the mean time the yolks of three fresh eggs, well beaten and strained, and mix the liquor with them by degrees. When all are well mixed, set the saucepan over a gentle fire, keeping a bason in one hand, to toss the sauce to and fro in, and shake the saucepan over the fire, that the eggs may not curdle. Do not let it boil, only make the sauce hot enough to give it the thickness of melted butter.—Fish sauce à la Craster, is made in the following manner. Thicken a quarter of a pound of butter with flour, and brown it. Add a pound of the best anchovies cut small, six blades of pounded mace, ten cloves, forty corns of black pepper and allspice, a few small onions, a faggot of sweet herbs, consisting of savoury, thyme, basil, and knotted marjoram, also a little parsley, and sliced horse-radish. On these pour half a pint of the best sherry, and a pint and a half of strong gravy. Simmer all gently for twenty minutes, then strain it through a sieve, and bottle it for use. The way of using it is, to boil some of it in the butter while melting.

FLANNELS. In order to make flannels keep their colour and not shrink, put them into a pail, and pour on boiling water. Let them lie till cold, before they are washed.

FLAT BEER. Much loss is frequently sustained from beer growing flat, during the time of drawing. To prevent this, suspend a pint or more of ground malt in it, tied up in a large bag, and keep the bung well closed. The beer will not then become vapid, but rather improve the whole time it is in use.

FLAT CAKES. Mix two pounds of flour, one pound of sugar, and one ounce of carraways, with four or five eggs, and a few spoonfuls of water. Make all into a stiff paste, roll it out thin, cut it into any shape, and bake on tins lightly floured. While baking, boil to a thin syrup a pound of sugar in a pint of water. When both are hot, dip each cake into the syrup, and place them on tins to dry in the oven for a short time. When the oven is a little cooler, return them into it, and let them remain there four or five hours. Cakes made in this way will keep good for a long time.

FLAT FISH. Flounders, plaice, soles, and other kinds of flat fish, are good boiled. Cut off the fins, draw and clean them well, dry them with a cloth, and boil them in salt and water. When the fins draw out easily, they are done enough. Serve them with shrimp, cockle, or mustard sauce, and garnish with red cabbage.

FLATULENCY. Wind in the stomach, accompanied with pain, is frequently occasioned by eating flatulent vegetables, or fat meat, with large draughts of beverage immediately afterwards, which turn rancid on the stomach; and of course, these ought to be avoided. Hot tea, turbid beer, and feculent liquors will have the same effect. A phlegmatic constitution, or costiveness, will render the complaint more frequent and painful. Gentle laxatives and a careful diet are the best remedy; but hot aromatics and spirituous liquors should be avoided.

FLEAS. Want of cleanliness remarkably contributes to the production of these offensive insects. The females of this tribe deposit their eggs in damp and filthy places, within the crevices of boards, and on rubbish, when they emerge in the form of fleas in about a month. Cleanliness, and frequent sprinkling of the room with a simple decoction of wormwood, will soon exterminate the whole breed of these disagreeable vermin; and the best remedy to expel them from bed clothes is a bag filled with dry moss, the odour of which is to them extremely offensive. Fumigation with brimstone, or the fresh leaves of pennyroyal sewed in a bag, and laid in the bed, will also have the desired effect. Dogs and cats may be effectually secured from the persecutions of these vermin, by occasionally anointing their skin with sweet oil, or oil of turpentine; or by rubbing into their coats some Scotch snuff. But if they be at all mangy, or their skin broken, the latter would be very painful and improper.

FLIES. If a room be swarming with these noisome insects, the most ready way of expelling them is to fumigate the apartment with the dried leaves of the gourd. If the window be opened, the smoke will instantly drive them out: or if the room be close, it will suffocate them. But in the latter case, no person should remain within doors, as the fume is apt to occasion the headache. Another way is to dissolve two drams of the extract of quassia in half a pint of boiling water; and, adding a little sugar or syrup, pour the mixture upon plates. The flies are extremely partial to this enticing food, and it never fails to destroy them. Camphor placed near any kind of provision will protect it from the flies.

FLIP. To make a quart of flip, put the ale on the fire to warm, and beat up three or four eggs, with four ounces of moist sugar. Add a tea-spoonful of grated nutmeg or ginger, and a quartern of good old rum or brandy. When the ale is nearly boiling, put it into one pitcher, and the rum and eggs into another: turn it from one pitcher to another, till it is as smooth as cream.

FLOATING ISLAND. Mix three half pints of thin cream with a quarter of a pint of raisin wine, a little lemon juice, orange flower water, and sugar. Put it into a dish for the middle of the table, and lay on with a spoon the following froth ready prepared. Sweeten half a pound of raspberry or currant jelly, add to it the whites of four eggs beaten, and beat up the jelly to a froth, until it will take any form you please. It should be raised high, to represent a castle or a rock.—Another way. Scald a codlin before it be ripe, or any other sharp apple, and pulp it through a sieve. Beat the whites of two eggs with sugar, and a spoonful of orange flower water; mix in the pulp by degrees, and beat all together till it produces a large quantity of froth. Serve it on a raspberry cream, or colour the froth with beet root, raspberry, or currant jelly, and set it on a white cream, which has already been flavoured with lemon, sugar, and raisin wine. The froth may also be laid on a custard.

FLOOR CLOTHS. The best are such as are painted on a fine cloth, well covered with colour, and where the flowers do not rise much above the ground, as they wear out first. The durability of the cloth will depend much on these two particulars, but more especially on the time it has been painted, and the goodness of the colours. If they have not been allowed sufficient space for becoming thoroughly hardened, a very little use will injure them: and as they are very expensive articles, care is necessary in preserving them. It answers to keep them some time before they are used, either hung up in a dry airy place, or laid down in a spare room. When taken up for the winter, they should be rolled round a carpet roller, and care taken not to crack the paint by turning in the edges too suddenly. Old carpets answer quite well, painted and seasoned some months before they are laid down. If intended for passages, the width must be directed when they are sent to the manufactory, as they are cut before painting.

FLOOR CLOTHS CLEANED. Sweep them first, then wipe them with a flannel; and when the dust and spots are removed, rub with a wax flannel, and dry them with a plain one. Use but little wax, and rub only with the latter to give a little smoothness, or it will make the floor cloth slippery, and endanger falling. Washing now and then with milk, after the above sweeping and dry rubbing, will give as good an appearance, and render the floor cloths less slippery.

FLOUNDERS. These are both sea and river fish: the Thames produces the best. They are in season from January to March, and from July to September. Their flesh should be thick and firm, and their eyes bright: they very soon become flabby and bad. Before they are dressed, they should be rubbed with salt inside and out, and lie two hours to acquire firmness. Then dip them in eggs, cover with grated bread, and fry them.

FLOUR. Good wheat flour may be known by the quantity of glutinous matter it contains, and which will appear when kneaded into dough. For this purpose take four ounces of fine flour, mix it with water, and work it together till it forms a thick paste. The paste is then to be well washed and kneaded with the hands under the water, and the water to be renewed till it ceases to become white by the operation. If the flour be sound, the paste which remains will be glutinous and elastic, and brittle after it has been baked.—Adulterated meal and flour are generally whiter and heavier than the good, and may be detected in a way similar to that already mentioned, under the article ADULTERATIONS. Or pour boiling water on some slices of bread, and drop on it some spirits of vitriol. Put them in the flour; and if it contain any quantity of whiting, chalk, or lime, a fermentation will ensue. Vitriol alone, dropped on adulterated bread or flour, will produce a similar effect.—American flour requires nearly twice as much water to make it into bread as is used for English flour, and therefore it is more profitable. Fourteen pounds of American flour will make twenty-one pounds and a half of bread, while the best sort of English flour produces only eighteen pounds and a half.

FLOUR CAUDLE. Into five large spoonfuls of pure water, rub smooth one dessert-spoonful of fine flour. Set over the fire five spoonfuls of new milk, and put into it two pieces of sugar. The moment it boils, pour into it the flour and water, and stir it over a slow fire twenty minutes. It is a nourishing and gently astringent food, and excellent for children who have weak bowels.

FLOWER GARDEN. The pleasures of the garden are ever various, ever new; and in every month of the year some attention is demanded, either in rearing the tender plant, in preparing the soil for its reception, or protecting the parent root from the severity of the winter's blast. Ranunculuses, anemones, tulips, and other bulbous roots, if not taken up, will be in great danger from the frost, and their shoots in the spring will either be impaired, or totally destroyed.——JANUARY. Cover the flower beds with wheat straw, to protect them from the cold; but where the shoots begin to appear, place behind them a reed edge, sloping three feet forward. A mat is to be let down from the top in severe weather, and taken up when it is mild. This will preserve them, without making them weak or sickly. The beds and boxes of seedling flowers should also be covered, and the fence removed when the weather is mild. Clean the auricula plants, pick off dead leaves, and scrape away the surface of the mould. Replenish them with some that is fine and fresh, set the pots up to the brim in the mould of a dry bed, and place behind them a reed edging. Cover carnation plants from wet, and defend them from mice and sparrows.——FEBRUARY. Make hotbeds for annual flowers, of the dung reserved for that purpose, and sow them upon a good thickness of mould, laid regularly over the dung. Transplant perennial flowers, and hardy shrubs, Canterbury bells, lilacs, and the like. Break up and new lay the gravel walks. Weed, rake, and clean the borders; and where the box of the edging is decayed, make it up with a fresh plantation. Sow auricula and polyanthus seeds in boxes, made of rough boards six inches deep, with holes at the bottom to run off the water. Fill the boxes with light mould, scatter the seeds thinly over the surface, sift some more mould over them about a quarter of an inch thick, and place them where they may enjoy the morning sun. Plant out carnations into pots for flowering.——MARCH. Watch the beds of tender flowers, and throw mats over them, supported by hoops, in hard weather. Continue transplanting all the perennial fibrous rooted flowers, such as golden-rods, and sweet-williams. Dig up the earth with a shovel about those which were planted in autumn, and clean the ground between them. All the pots of flowering plants must now be dressed. Pick off dead leaves, remove the earth at the top, and put fresh instead; then give them a gentle watering, and set them in their places for flowering. Be careful that the roots are not wounded, and repeat the watering once in three days. The third week in March is the time to sow sweet peas, poppies, catchflies, and all the hardy annual plants. The last week is proper for transplanting evergreens, and a showery day should be chosen for the purpose. Hotbeds should now be made, to receive the seedlings of annual flowers raised in the former bed.——APRIL. Tie up to sticks the stalks of tall flowers, cut the sticks about two feet long, thrust them eight inches into the ground, and hide them among the leaves. Clean and rake the ground between them. Take off the slips of auriculas, and plant them out carefully for an increase. Transplant perennial flowers and evergreens, as in the former months; take up the roots of colchichams, and other autumnal bulbous plants. Sow French honeysuckles, wallflowers, and other hardy plants, upon the natural ground, and the more tender sorts on hotbeds. Transplant those sown last month, into the second hotbed. Sow carnations and pinks on the natural ground, and on open borders.——MAY. When the leaves of sowbreads are decayed, take up the roots, and lay them by carefully till the time of planting. Take up the hyacinth roots which have done flowering, and lay them sideways in a bed of dry rich mould, leaving the stems and leaves to die away: this will greatly strengthen the roots. Roll the gravel walks carefully and frequently, and keep the grass clean mowed. Clean all the borders from weeds, take off the straggling branches from the large flowering plants, and train them up in a handsome shape. Plant out French and African marigolds from the hotbeds, with other autumnals, the last week of this month, choosing a cloudy warm day. Tie up the stalks of carnations, pot the tender annuals, such as balsams and amaranths, and set them in a hotbed frame, till summer is more advanced for planting them in the open ground.——JUNE. Choose the evening of a mild showery day, and plant out into the open ground, the tender annuals hitherto kept in pots in the hotbed frame. They must be carefully loosened from the sides of the pot, and taken out with all the mould about them; a large hole must be opened for each, to set them upright in it; and when settled in the ground by gentle watering, they must be tied up to sticks. Let pinks, carnations, and sweet-williams, be laid this month for an increase. Let the layers be covered lightly, and gently watered every other day. Spring flowers being now over, and their leaves faded, the roots must be taken up, and laid by for planting again at a proper season. Snow-drops, winter-aconite, and such sorts, are to be thus managed. The hyacinth roots, laid flat in the ground, must now be taken up, and the dead leaves clipped off; and when cleared from the mould, they must be spread upon a mat in an airy room to dry, and laid by for future planting. Tulip roots also must now be taken up, as the leaves decay: anemones and ranunculuses are treated in the same manner. Cut in three or four places, the cups or poles of the carnations that are near blowing, that they may show regularly. At the same time inoculate some of the fine kind of roses.——JULY. Clip box edgings, cut and trim hedges, look over all the borders, clear them from weeds, and stir up the mould between the plants. Roll the gravel frequently, and mow the grass plats. Inoculate roses and jasmines that require this kind of propagation, and any of the other flowering shrubs. Gather the seeds of flowers intended to be propagated, and lay them upon a shelf in an airy room in the pods. When they are well hardened, tie them up in paper bags, but do not take them out of the pods till they are wanted. Lay pinks and sweet-williams in the earth as formerly, cut down the stalks of those plants which have done flowering, and which are not kept for seed. Tie up with sticks such as are coming into flower, as for the earlier kinds. Sow lupins, larkspurs, and similar sorts, on dry warm borders, to stand the winter, and flower early next year.—— AUGUST. Dig up a mellow border, and draw lines at five inches distance, lengthways and across. In the centre of these squares, plant the seedling polyanthuses, one in each square. In the same manner plant out the seedling auriculas. Shade them till they have taken root, and water them once a day. See whether the layers of sweet-williams, carnations, and such like, have taken root; transplant such as are rooted, and give frequent gentle waterings to the others in order to promote it. Cut down the stalks of plants that have done flowering, saving the seed that may be wanted, as it ripens, and water the tender annuals every evening. Sow anemones and ranunculuses, tulip, and narcissus seed. Dig up a border for early tulip roots, and others for hyacinths, anemones, and ranunculuses. Sow annuals to stand through the winter, and shift auriculas into fresh pots.——SEPTEMBER. During this month, preparation should be made for the next season. Tear up the annuals that have done flowering, and cut down such perennials as are past their beauty. Bring in other perennials from the nursery beds, and plant them with care at regular distances. Take up the box edgings where they have outgrown their proper size, and part and plant them afresh. Plant tulip and other flower roots, slip polyanthuses, and place them in rich shady borders. Sow the seeds of flower de luce and crown imperial, as also of auriculas and polyanthuses, according to the method before recommended. Part off the roots of flower de luce, piony, and others of a similar kind. In the last week transplant hardy flowering shrubs, and they will be strong the next summer.——OCTOBER. Let all the bulbous roots for spring flowering be put into the ground; narcissus, maragon, tulips, and such ranunculuses and anemones as were not planted sooner. Transplant columbines, monkshood, and all kinds of fibrous rooted perennials. Place under shelter the auriculas and carnations that are in pots. Dig up a dry border, and if not dry enough, dig in some sand, and set in the pots up to the brim. Place the reed fence sloping behind them, and fasten a mat to its top, that may be let down in bad weather. Take off the dead leaves of the auriculas, before they are thus planted. Bring into the garden some fresh flowering shrubs, wherever they may be wanted, and at the end of the month prune some of the hardier kind. ——NOVEMBER. Prepare a good heap of pasture ground, with the turf among it, to rot into mould for the borders. Transplant honeysuckles and spireas, with other hardy flowering shrubs. Rake over the beds of seedling flowers, and strew some peas straw over to keep out the frost. Cut down the stems of perennials which have done flowering, pull up annuals that are spent, and rake and clear the ground. Place hoops over the beds of ranunculuses and anemones, and lay mats or cloths in readiness to draw over them, in case of hard rains or frost. Clean up the borders in all parts of the garden, and take care to destroy not only the weeds, but all kinds of moss. Look over the seeds of those flowers which were gathered in summer, to see that they are dry and sweet; and prepare a border or two for the hardier kind, by digging and cleaning.——DECEMBER. During frost or cold rain, draw the mats and cloths over the ranunculuses; give the anemones a little air in the middle of every tolerable day; and as soon as possible, uncover them all day, but draw on the mats at night. Throw up the earth where flowering shrubs are to be planted in the spring, and turn it once a fortnight. Dig up the borders that are to receive flower roots in the spring, and give them the advantage of a fallow, by throwing up the ground in a ridge. Scatter over it a very little rotten dung from a melon bed, and afterwards turn it twice during the winter. Examine the flowering shrubs, and prune them. Cut away all the dead wood, shorten luxuriant branches, and if any cross each other, take away one. Leave them so that the air may have a free passage between them. Sift a quarter of an inch of good fresh mould over the roots of perennial flowers, whose stalks have been cut down, and then rake over the borders. This will give the whole an air of culture and good management, which is always pleasing.

FLOWER POTS. As flowers and plants should enjoy a free circulation of air to make them grow well, sitting rooms are not very well adapted to the purpose, unless they could be frequently ventilated by opening the doors and windows. In every severe frost or damp weather, moderate fires should be made in the rooms where the plants are placed, and the shutters closed at night. Placing saucers under the pots, and pouring water continually into them, is highly improper: it should be poured on the mould, that it may filter through it, and thereby refresh the fibres of the plant. Many kinds of annuals, sown in March and the beginning of April, may be transplanted into pots about the end of May, and should be frequently watered till they have taken root. If transplanted in the summer season, the evening is the proper time, and care must be taken not to break the fibres of the root. When the plants are attacked by any kind of crawling insects, the evil may be prevented by keeping the saucers full of water, so as to form a river round the pot, and rubbing some oil round the side. Oil is fatal to most kinds of insects, and but few of them can endure it.

FLOWER SEEDS. When the seeds begin to ripen they should be supported with sticks, to prevent their being scattered by the wind; and in wet weather they should be removed to a dry place, and rubbed out when convenient. August is in general the proper time for gathering flower seeds, but many kinds will ripen much sooner. To ascertain whether the seed be fully ripe, put a little of it into water: if it be come to maturity, it will sink to the bottom, and if not it will swim upon the surface. To preserve them for vegetation, it is only necessary to wrap the seed up in cartridge paper, pasted down and varnished over with gum, or the white of an egg. Some kinds of seeds are best enclosed in sealing wax.

FLUMMERY. Steep in cold water, for a day and a night, three large handfuls of very fine white oatmeal. Pour it off clear, add as much more water, and let it stand the same time. Strain it through a fine hair sieve, and boil it till it is as thick as hasty pudding, stirring it well all the time. When first strained, put to it one large spoonful of white sugar, and two of orange flower water. Pour it into shallow dishes, and serve it up with wine, cider, and milk; or it will be very good with cream and sugar.

FOMENTATIONS. Boil two ounces each of camomile flowers, and the tops of wormwood, in two quarts of water. Pour off the liquor, put it on the fire again, dip in a piece of flannel, and apply it to the part as hot as the patient can bear it. When it grows cold, heat it up again, dip in another piece of flannel, apply it as the first, and continue changing them as often as they get cool, taking care not to let the air get to the part affected when the flannel is changed.—To relieve the toothache, pain in the face, or any other acute pain, the following anodyne fomentation may be applied. Take two ounces of white poppy heads, and half an ounce of elder flowers, and boil them in three pints of water, till it is reduced one third. Strain off the liquor, and foment the part affected.

FOOD. In the early ages of the world, mankind were chiefly supported by berries, roots, and such other vegetables as the earth produced of itself, according to the original grant of the great Proprietor of all things. In later ages, especially after the flood, this grant was enlarged; and man had recourse to animals, as well as to vegetables artificially raised for their support, while the art of preparing food has been brought to the highest degree of perfection. Vegetables are however, with a few exceptions, more difficult of digestion than animal food; but a due proportion of both, with the addition of acids, is the most conducive to health, as well as agreeable to the palate. Animal as well as vegetable food may be rendered unwholesome by being kept too long; and when offensive to the senses, they become alike injurious to health. Diseased animals, and such as die of themselves, ought never to be eaten. Such as are fed grossly, stalled cattle and pigs, without any exercise, do not afford food so nourishing or wholesome as others. Salt meat is not so easily digested as fresh provisions, and has a tendency to produce putrid diseases, especially the scurvy. If vegetables and milk were more used, there would be less scurvy, and fewer inflammatory fevers. Our food ought neither to be too moist, nor too dry. Liquid food relaxes and renders the body feeble: hence those who live much on tea, and other watery diet, generally become weak, and unable to digest solid food. They are also liable to hysterics, with a train of other nervous affections. But if the food be too dry, it disposes the body to inflammatory disorders, and is equally to be avoided. Families would do well to prepare their own diet and drink, as much as possible, in order to render it good and wholesome. Bread in particular is so necessary a part of daily food, that too much care cannot be taken to see that it be made of sound grain duly prepared, and kept from all unwholesome ingredients. Those who make bread for sale, seek rather to please the eye than to promote health. The best bread is that which is neither too coarse nor too fine, well fermented, and made of wheat flour, or wheat and rye mixed together. Good fermented liquors, neither too weak nor too strong, are to be preferred. If too weak, they require to be drunk soon, and then they produce wind and flatulencies in the stomach. If kept too long, they turn sour, and then become unwholesome. On the other hand, strong liquor, by hurting the digestion, tends to weaken and relax: it also keeps up a constant fever, which exhausts the spirits, inflames the blood, and disposes the body to numberless diseases. Beer, cider, and other family liquors, should be of such strength as to keep till they are ripe, and then they should be used. Persons of a weak and relaxed habit should avoid every thing hard of digestion: their diet requires to be light and nourishing, and they should take sufficient exercise in the open air. Those who abound with blood, should abstain from rich wines and highly nourishing food, and live chiefly on vegetables. Corpulent persons ought frequently to use radish, garlic, or such things as promote perspiration. Their drink should be tea, coffee, or the like; they ought also to take much exercise, and but little sleep. Those who are of a thin habit, should follow the opposite course. Such as are troubled with sour risings in the stomach, should live chiefly on animal food; and those who are afflicted with hot risings and heartburn, should have a diet of acid vegetables. Persons of low spirits, and subject to nervous disorders, should avoid all flatulent food, whatever is hard of digestion, or apt to turn sour on the stomach. Their diet should be light, cool, and of an opening nature; not only suited to the age and constitution, but also to the manner of life. A sedentary person should live more sparingly than one who labours hard without doors, and those who are afflicted with any particular disease ought to avoid such aliment as has a tendency to increase it. Those afflicted with the gravel ought to avoid every thing astringent; and the scorbutic of every description, salted or smoked provisions. In the first period of life, the food should be light, but nourishing, and frequently taken. For infants in particular, it ought to be adapted to their age, and the strength of their digestive powers. No food whatever that has been prepared for many hours should be given them, especially after being warmed up; for it creates flatulence, heartburn, and a variety of other disorders. Sudden changes from liquid to solid food should be avoided, as well as a multiplicity of different kinds; and all stimulating dishes and heating liquors, prepared for adults, should be carefully withheld from children. The common but indecent practice of introducing chewed victuals into their mouth, is equally disgusting and unwholesome. Solid food is most proper for the state of manhood, but it ought not to be too uniform. Nature has provided a great variety for the use of man, and given him an appetite suited to that variety: the constant use of one kind of food therefore is not good for the constitution, though any great or sudden change in diet ought as well to be avoided. The change should be gradual, as any sudden transition from a low to a rich and luxurious mode of living, may endanger health, and even life itself. The diet suited to the last period of life, when nature is on the decline, approaches nearly to that of the first: it should be light and nourishing, and more frequently taken than in vigorous age. Old people are generally afflicted with wind, giddiness, and headachs, which are frequently occasioned by fasting too long, and even many sudden deaths arise from the same cause. The stomach therefore should never be allowed in any case to be too long empty, but especially in the decline of life. Proper attention to diet is of the utmost importance, not only to the preservation of health, but in the cure of many diseases, which may be effected by diet only. Its effects indeed are not always so quick as those of medicine, but they are generally more lasting, and are obtained with greater ease and certainty. Temperance and exercise are the two best physicians in the world; and if they were duly regarded, there would be little occasion for any other.

FOOD FOR BIRDS. An excellent food for linnets, canaries, and other singing birds, may be prepared in the following manner. Knead together one pound of split peas ground to flour, half a pound each of coarse sugar and fine grated bread, two ounces of unsalted butter, and the yolks of two eggs. Brown the paste gently in a fryingpan, and when cold mix with it two ounces of mace seed, and two pounds of bruised hemp seed, separated from the husk. This paste given to birds in small quantities will preserve them in health, and prompt them to sing every month in the year.

FORCEMEAT. This article, whether in the form of stuffing balls, or for patties, makes a considerable part of good cooking, by the flavour it imparts to whatsoever dish it may be added. Yet at many tables, where every thing else is well done, it is common to find very bad stuffing. Exact rules for the quantity cannot easily be given; but the following observations may be useful, and habit will soon give knowledge in mixing it to the taste. The selection of ingredients should of course be made, according to what they are wanted for, observing that of the most pungent, the smallest quantity should be used. No one flavour should greatly preponderate; yet if several dishes be served the same day, there should be a marked variety in the taste of the forcemeat, as well as of the gravies. It should be consistent enough to cut with a knife, but neither dry nor heavy. The following are the articles of which forcemeat may be made, without giving it any striking flavour. Cold fowl or veal, scraped ham, fat bacon, beef suet, crumbs of bread, salt, white pepper, parsley, nutmeg, yolk and white of eggs well beaten to bind the mixture. To these, any of the following may be added, to vary the taste, and give it a higher relish. Oysters, anchovy, taragon, savoury, pennyroyal, knotted marjoram, thyme, basil, yolks of hard eggs, cayenne, garlic, shalot, chives, Jamaica pepper in fine powder, or two or three cloves.

FORCEMEAT BALLS. To make fine forcemeat balls for fish soups, or stewed fish, beat together the flesh and soft parts of a lobster, half an anchovy, a large piece of boiled celery, the yolk of a hard egg, a little cayenne, mace, salt, and white pepper. Add two table-spoonfuls of bread crumbs, one of oyster liquor, two ounces of warmed butter, and two eggs well beaten. Make the whole into balls, and fry them in butter, of a fine brown.

FORCEMEAT FOR FOWLS. Shred a little ham or gammon, some cold veal or fowl, beef suet, parsley, a small quantity of onion, and a very little lemon peel. Add salt, nutmeg, or pounded mace, bread crumbs, and either white pepper or cayenne. Pound it all together in a mortar, and bind it with one or two eggs beaten and strained. The same stuffing will do for meat, or for patties. For fowls, it is usually put between the skin and the flesh.

FORCEMEAT FOR GOOSE. Chop very fine about two ounces of onion, and an ounce of green sage. Add four ounces of bread crumbs, the yolk and white of an egg, a little pepper and salt; and if approved, a minced apple. This will do for either goose or duck stuffing.

FORCEMEAT FOR HARE. Chop up the liver, with an anchovy, some fat bacon, a little suet, some sweet herbs, and an onion. Add salt, pepper, nutmeg, crumbs of bread, and an egg to bind all together.

FORCEMEAT FOR SAVOURY PIES. The same as for fowls, only substituting fat or bacon, instead of suet. If the pie be of rabbit or fowls, the livers mixed with fat and lean pork, instead of bacon, will make an excellent stuffing. The seasoning is to be the same as for fowls or meat.

FORCEMEAT FOR TURKEY. The same stuffing will do for boiled or roast turkey as for veal, or to make it more relishing, add a little grated ham or tongue, an anchovy, or the soft part of a dozen oysters. Pork sausage meat is sometimes used to stuff turkies or fowls, or fried, and sent up as garnish.

FORCEMEAT FOR TURTLE. A pound of fine fresh suet, one ounce of cold veal or chicken, chopped fine; crumbs of bread, a little shalot or onion, white pepper, salt, nutmeg, mace, pennyroyal, parsley, and lemon thyme, finely shred. Beat as many fresh eggs, yolks and whites separately, as will make the above ingredients into a moist paste. Roll it into small balls, and boil them in fresh lard, putting them in just as it boils up. When of a light brown take them out, and drain them before the fire. If the suet be moist or stale, a great many more eggs will be necessary. Balls made in this way are remarkably light; but being greasy, some people prefer them with less suet and eggs.

FORCEMEAT FOR VEAL. Scrape two ounces of undressed lean veal, free from skin and sinews; two ounces of beef or veal suet, and two of bread crumbs. Chop fine two drams of parsley, one of lemon peel, one of sweet herbs, one of onion, and add half a dram of mace or allspice reduced to a fine powder. Pound all together in a mortar, break into it the yolk and white of an egg, rub it all up well together, and season it with a little pepper and salt. This may be made more savoury, by the addition of cold boiled tongue, anchovy, shalot, cayenne, or curry powder.

FOREHAND OF PORK. Cut out the bone, sprinkle the inside with salt, pepper, and dried sage. Roll the pork tight, and tie it up; warm a little butter to baste it, and then flour it. Roast it by a hanging jack, and about two hours will do it.

FOREQUARTER OF LAMB. Roast it either whole, or in separate parts. If left to be cold, chopped parsley should be sprinkled over it. The neck and breast together are called a scoven.

FOWLS. In purchasing fowls for dressing, it is necessary to see that they are fresh and good. If a cock bird is young, his spurs will be short; but be careful to observe that they have not been cut or pared, which is a trick too often practised. If fresh, the vent will be close and dark. Pullets are best just before they begin to lay, and yet are full of egg. If hens are old, their combs and legs will be rough: if young, they will be smooth. A good capon has a thick belly and a large rump: there is a particular fat at his breast, and the comb is very pale. Black-legged fowls being moist, are best for roasting.

FRECKLES. The cosmetics generally recommended for improving the skin and bloom of the face are highly pernicious, and ought by no means to be employed. Temperance in diet and exercise, with frequent washing and bathing, are the best means of preserving a healthful countenance. But those who desire to soften and improve the skin, may use an infusion of horseradish in milk, or the expressed juice of houseleek mixed with cream, which will be useful and inoffensive. Freckles on the face, or small discolourations on other parts of the skin, are constitutional in some cases; and in others, they are occasioned by the action of the sun upon the part, and frequent exposures to the morning air. For dispersing them, take four ounces of lemon juice, one dram of powdered borax, and two drams of sugar: mix them together, and let them stand a few days in a glass bottle till the liquid is fit for use, and then rub it on the face. But for chaps and flaws in the skin, occasioned by cold, rub on a little plain unscented pomatum at bed-time, and let it remain till morning. Or, which is much better, anoint the face with honey water, made to the consistence of cream, which will form a kind of varnish on the skin, and protect it from the effects of cold.

FRENCH BEANS. String, and cut them into four parts; if smaller, they look so much the better. Lay them in salt and water; and when the water boils, put them in with some salt. As soon as they are done, serve them immediately, to preserve their colour. Or when half done, drain off the water, and add two spoonfuls of broth strained. In finishing them, put in a little cream, with flour and butter.

FRENCH BREAD. With a quarter of a peck of fine flour, mix the yolks of three and the whites of two eggs, beaten and strained; a little salt, half a pint of good yeast that is not bitter, and as much lukewarm milk as will work it into a thin light dough. Stir it about, but do not knead it. Divide the dough into three parts, put them into wooden dishes, set them to rise, then turn them out into the oven, which must be quick, and rasp the bread when done.

FRENCH DUMPLINGS. Grate a penny loaf, add half a pound of currants, three quarters of a pound of beef suet finely shred, and half a grated nutmeg. Beat up the yolks of three eggs with three spoonfuls of cream, as much white wine, and a little sugar. Mix all together, work it up into a paste, make it into dumplings of a convenient size, and tie them up in cloths. Put them into boiling water, and let them boil three quarters of an hour.

FRENCH PIE. Lay a puff paste round the edge of the dish, and put in either slices of veal, rabbits or chickens jointed; with forcemeat balls, sweetbreads cut in pieces, artichoke bottoms, and a few truffles.

FRENCH PORRIDGE. Stir together some oatmeal and water, and pour off the latter. Put fresh in, stir it well, and let it stand till the next day. Strain it through a fine sieve, and boil the water, which must be small in quantity, adding some milk while it is doing. With the addition of toast, this is much in request abroad, for the breakfast of weakly persons.

FRENCH PUDDING. Grate six ounces of brown bread, and shred half a pound of suet. Add four eggs well beaten, half a pound of currants picked and washed, a quarter of a pound of sugar, and a little nutmeg. Mix all together, tie the pudding up close in a cloth, and boil it two hours. Serve it up with a sauce of melted butter, a little sugar and sweet wine.

FRENCH ROLLS. Rub one ounce of butter into a pound of flour; mix one egg beaten, a little yeast that is not bitter, and as much milk as will make the dough tolerably stiff. Beat it well, but do not knead it: let it rise, and bake it on tins.

FRENCH SALAD. Mince up three anchovies, a shalot, and some parsley. Put them into a bowl with two table-spoonfuls of vinegar, one of oil, and a little salt and mustard. When well mixed, add by degrees some cold roast or boiled meat in very thin slices: put in a few at a time, not exceeding two or three inches long. Shake them in the seasoning, and then put more: cover the bowl close, and let the salad be prepared three hours before it is to be eaten. Garnish with parsley, and a few slices of the fat.

FRICANDEAU OF BEEF. Take a nice piece of lean beef; lard it with bacon seasoned with pepper, salt, cloves, mace, and allspice. Put it into a stewpan with a pint of broth, a glass of white wine, a bundle of parsley, all sorts of sweet herbs, a clove of garlic, a shalot or two, four cloves, pepper and salt. When the meat is become tender, cover it close. Skim the sauce well, strain it, set it on the fire, and let it boil till reduced to a glaze. Glaze the larded side with this, and serve the meat on sorrel sauce.

FRICANDEAU OF VEAL. Cut a large piece from the fat side of the leg, about nine inches long and half as thick and broad. Beat it with the rolling pin, take off the skin, and trim the rough edges. Lard the top and sides, cover it with fat bacon, and then with white paper. Lay it into a stewpan with any pieces of undressed veal or mutton, four onions, a sliced carrot, a faggot of sweet herbs, four blades of mace, four bay leaves, a pint of good veal or mutton broth, and four or five ounces of lean ham or gammon. Cover the pan close, and let it stew slowly for three hours; then take up the meat, remove all the fat from the gravy, and boil it quick to a glaze. Keep the fricandeau quite hot, and then glaze it. Serve it with the remainder of the glaze in the dish, and sorrel sauce in a tureen.—The following is a cheaper way of making a good fricandeau of veal. With a sharp knife cut the lean part of a large neck from the best end, scooping it from the bones a hand's length, and prepare it in the manner above directed. Three or four bones only will be necessary, and they will make the gravy; but if the prime part of the leg is cut off, it spoils the whole.—Another way is to take two large round sweetbreads, and prepare them like veal. Make a rich gravy with truffles, morels, mushrooms, and artichoke bottoms, and serve it round.

FRICASSEE OF CHICKENS. Boil rather more than half, in a small quantity of water, and let them cool. Cut them up, simmer in a little gravy made of the liquor they were boiled in, adding a bit of veal or mutton, onion, mace, lemon peel, white pepper, and a bunch of sweet herbs. When quite tender, keep them hot, while the following sauce is prepared. Strain off the liquor, return it into the saucepan with a little salt, a scrape of nutmeg, and a little flour and butter. Give it one boil, and when ready to serve, beat up the yolk of an egg, add half a pint of cream, and stir them over the fire, but do not let it boil. It will be quite as good however without the egg. Without the addition of any other meat, the gravy may be made of the trimmings of the fowls, such as the necks, feet, small wing bones, gizzards, and livers.

FRICASSEE OF RABBITS. Skin them, cut them in pieces, soak in warm water, and clean them. Then stew them in a little fresh water, with a bit of lemon peel, a little white wine, an anchovy, an onion, two cloves, and a sprig of sweet herbs. When tender take them out, strain off the liquor, put a very little of it into a quarter of a pint of thick cream, with a piece of butter, and a little flour. Keep it constantly stirring till the butter is melted; then put in the rabbit, with a little grated lemon peel, mace, and lemon juice. Shake all together over the fire, and make it quite hot. If more agreeable, pickled mushrooms may be used instead of lemon.—To make a brown fricassee, prepare the rabbits as above, and fry them in butter to a nice brown. Put some gravy or beef broth into the pan, shake in some flour, and keep it stirring over the fire. Add some ketchup, a very little shalot chopped, salt, cayenne, and lemon juice, or pickled mushrooms. Boil it up, put in the rabbit, and shake it round till it is quite hot.

FRYING. This is often a very convenient and expeditious mode of cooking; but though one of the most common, it is as commonly performed in a very imperfect manner, and meets with less attention than the comfort of a good meal requires. A fryingpan should be about four inches deep, with a perfectly flat and thick bottom, and perpendicular sides. When used it should be half filled with fat, for good frying is in fact, boiling in fat. To make sure that the pan is quite clean, rub a little fat over it, then make it warm, and wipe it out with a clean cloth. Great care must be taken in frying, never to use any oil, butter, lard, or drippings, but what is quite clean, fresh, and free from salt. Any thing dirty spoils the appearance, any thing bad tasted or stale spoils the flavour, and salt prevents its browning. Fine olive oil is the most delicate for frying, but it is very expensive, and bad oil spoils every thing that is dressed with it. For general purposes, and especially for fish, clean fresh lard is not near so expensive as oil or clarified butter, and does almost as well, except for collops and cutlets. Butter often burns before any one is aware, and what is fried with it will get a dark and dirty appearance. Dripping, if nicely clean and fresh, is almost as good as any thing: if not clean, it may easily be clarified. Whatever fat be used, let it remain in the pan a few minutes after frying, and then pour it through a sieve into a clean bason. If not burnt, it will be found much better than it was at first; but the fat in which fish has been fried, will not serve any other purpose. To fry fish, parsley, potatoes, or any thing that is watery, the fire must be very clear, and the fat quite hot, which will be the case when it has done hissing. Fish will neither be firm nor crisp, nor of a good colour, unless the fat be of a proper heat. To determine this, throw a little bit of bread into the pan: if it fries crisp, the fat is ready: if it burns the bread, it is too hot. Whatever is fried before the fat is hot enough, will be pale and sodden, and offend the palate and the stomach, as well as the eye. The fat also must be thoroughly drained from the fry, especially from such things as are dressed in bread crumbs, or the flavour will be impaired. The dryness of fish depends much upon its having been fried in fat of a due degree of heat, they are then crisp and dry in a few minutes after being taken out of the pan: when they are not, lay them on a soft cloth before the fire, and turn them till they are dry.

FRIED CARP. Scale, draw, and wash them clean; dry them in flour, and fry them in hog's lard to a light brown. Fry some toast, cut three-corner ways, with the roes; lay the fish on a coarse cloth to drain, and serve them up with butter, anchovy sauce, and the juice of a lemon. Garnish with the bread, roe, and lemon.

FRIED EELS. There is a greater difference in the goodness of eels than of any other fish. The true silver-eel, so called from the bright colour of the belly, is caught in the Thames. The Dutch eels sold at Billingsgate are very bad; those taken in great floods are generally good, but in ponds they have usually a strong rank flavour. Except the middle of summer, they are always in season. If small, they should be curled round and fried, being first dipped into eggs and crumbs of bread.

FRIED EGGS. Boil six eggs for three minutes, put them in cold water, and take off the shells, without breaking the whites. Wrap the eggs up in a puff paste, smear them over with egg, and grate some bread over them. Put into a stewpan a sufficient quantity of lard or butter to swim the eggs; and when the lard is hot, put in the eggs, and fry them of a good colour. Lay them on a cloth to drain.

FRIED HERBS. Clean and drain a good quantity of spinach leaves, two large handfuls of parsley, and a handful of green onions. Chop the parsley and onions, and sprinkle them among the spinach. Stew them together with a little salt, and a bit of butter the size of a walnut. Shake the pan when it begins to grow warm, and let it lie closely covered over a slow stove till done enough. It is served with slices of broiled calves' liver, small rashers of bacon, and fried eggs. The latter on the herbs, and the other in a separate dish. This is the mode of dressing herbs in Staffordshire.

FRIED MACKAREL. Stuff the fish with grated bread, minced parsley and lemon peel, pepper and salt, nutmeg, and the yolk of an egg, all mixed together. Serve with anchovy and fennel sauce. Or split the fish open, cut off their heads, season and hang them up four or five hours, and then broil them. Make the sauce of fennel and parsley chopped fine, and mixed with melted butter.

FRIED OYSTERS. To prepare a garnish for boiled fish, make a batter of flour, milk, and eggs. Season it a very little, dip the oysters into the batter, and fry them of a fine yellow brown. A little nutmeg should be put into the seasoning, and a few crumbs of bread into the flour.

FRIED PARSLEY. Pick some young parsley very clean, and put it into a fryingpan with a bit of butter. Stir it with a knife till it becomes crisp, and use it for garnishing. Or rub the picked parsley in a cloth to clean it, and set it before the fire in a Dutch oven till it is crisp. This is better than fried parsley, and may be rubbed on steaks, calf's liver, or any other dish of the kind.

FRIED PATTIES. Mince a bit of cold veal, and six oysters; mix them with a few crumbs of bread, salt, pepper, and nutmeg, and a very small bit of lemon peel. Add the liquor of the oysters, warm all together in a tosser, but it must not boil, and then let it grow cold. Prepare a good puff-paste, roll it thin, and cut it into round or square pieces. Put some of the mixture between two of them, twist the edges to keep in the gravy, and fry them of a fine brown. If baked, it becomes a fashionable dish. All patties should be washed over with egg before they are baked.

FRIED POTATOES. Slice them thin, and fry them in butter till they are brown; then lay them in a dish, and pour melted butter over them. Potatoes may likewise be fried in butter, and served up with powder sugar strewed over them. Any kind of fruit may be fried in the same manner, and all batter should be fried in hog's lard.

FRIED RABBIT. Cut it into joints, and fry it in butter of a nice brown. Send it to table with fried or dried parsley, and gravy or liver sauce.

FRIED SMELTS. Wipe them clean, take away the gills, rub them over with a feather dipped in egg, and strew on some grated bread. Fry them in hog's lard over a clear fire, and put them in when the fat is boiling hot. When they are of a fine brown, take them out and drain off the fat. Garnish with fried parsley and lemon.

FRIED SOLES. Divide two or three soles from the backbone, and take off the head, fins, and tail. Sprinkle the inside with salt, roll them up tight from the tail and upwards, and fasten with small skewers. Small fish do not answer, but if large or of a tolerable size, put half a fish in each roll. Dip them into yolks of eggs, and cover them with crumbs. Egg them over again, and then put more crumbs. Fry them of a beautiful colour in lard, or in clarified butter. Or dip the soles in egg, and cover them with fine crumbs of bread. Set on a fryingpan of the proper size, and put into it a good quantity of fresh lard or dripping. Let it boil, and immediately put the fish into it, and do them of a fine brown. Soles that have been fried, eat good cold with oil, vinegar, salt and mustard.

FRIED TENCH. Scale and clean the fish well, dry and lay them before the fire, dust them with flour, and fry them in dripping or hog's lard. Serve with crisped parsley, and plain butter. Perch, trout, and grayling may be done the same.

FRIED TURBOT. Cut a small turbot across in ribs, dry and flour it, put it into a fryingpan, and cover it with boiling lard. Fry it brown, and drain it. Clean the pan, put in a little wine, an anchovy, salt, nutmeg, and a little ginger. Put in the fish, and stew it till the liquor is half wasted. Then take it out, put in some butter rolled in flour, with a minced lemon, and simmer them to a proper thickness. Rub a hot dish with a piece of shalot, lay the turbot in the dish, and pour the sauce over it.

FRIED VENISON. Cut the meat into slices, fry it of a bright brown, and keep it hot before the fire. Make gravy of the bones, add a little butter rolled in flour, stir it in the pan till it is thick and brown, and put in some port and lemon juice. Warm the venison in it, put in the dish, and pour the sauce over it. Send up currant jelly in a glass.

FRITTERS. Make them of pancake batter, dropped in small quantities into the pan: or put apple into batter, pared and sliced, and fry some of it with each slice. Currants, or very thinly-sliced lemon, make an agreeable change. Fritters for company should be served on a folded napkin in the dish. Any sort of sweetmeat, or ripe fruit, may be made into fritters.

FRONTINIAC. Boil twelve pounds of loaf sugar, and six pounds of raisins cut small, in six gallons of water. When the liquor is almost cold, put in half a peck of elder flowers; and the next day six spoonfuls of the syrup of lemons, and four of yeast. Let it stand two days, put it into a barrel that will just hold it, and bottle it after it has stood about two months.

FROST AND BLIGHTS. When a fruit tree is in full blossom, the best way to preserve it from frost and blights is to twine a rope upon its branches, and bring the end of it into a pail of water. If a light frost happen in the night, the tree will not be affected by it; but an ice will be formed on the surface of the water, in which the end of the rope is immersed. This experiment may easily be tried on wall fruit, and has been found to answer. If trees be infected with an easterly blight, the best way is to fumigate them with brimstone strewed on burning charcoal: this will effectually destroy the insects, and preserve the fruit. Afterwards it will be proper to dash them with water, or wash the branches with a woollen cloth, and clear them of all glutinous matter and excrescences of every kind, which would harbour the insects; but the washing should be performed in the early part of a warm day, that the moisture may be exhaled before the cold of the evening approaches.

FROSTED POTATOES. If soaked three hours in cold water, before they are to be prepared as food, changing the water every hour, these valuable roots will recover their salubrious quality and flavour. While in cold water, they must stand where a sufficiency of artificial heat may prevent freezing. If much frozen, allow a quarter of an ounce of saltpetre to every peck of potatoes, and dissolve it in the water. But if so much penetrated by the frost as to render them unfit for culinary purposes, they may be made into starch, and will yield a large quantity of flour for that purpose.

FROTH FOR CREAMS. Sweeten half a pound of the pulp of damsons, or any other scalded fruit. Put to it the whites of four eggs beaten, and beat up the pulp with them till it will stand up, and take any form. It should be rough, to imitate a rock, or the billows of the ocean. This froth looks and eats well, and may be laid on cream, custard, or trifle, with a spoon.

FRUIT. The method of preserving any kind of fruit all the year, is to put them carefully into a wide-mouthed glass vessel, closed down with oiled paper. The glasses are to be placed in a box filled with a mixture of four pounds of dry sand, two pounds of bole-armeniac, and one pound of saltpetre, so that the fruit may be completely covered. The fruit should be gathered by the hand before it be thoroughly ripe, and the box kept in a dry place.

FRUIT BISCUITS. To the pulp of any scalded fruit, put an equal weight of sugar sifted, and beat it two hours. Then make it into little white-paper forms, dry them in a cool oven, and turn them the next day. They may be put into boxes in the course of two or three days.

FRUIT FOR CHILDREN. To prepare fruit for children, far more wholesome than in puddings or pies, put some sliced apples, plums or gooseberries, into a stone jar, and sprinkle among them a sufficient quantity of fine moist sugar. Set the jar on a hot hearth, or in a saucepan of boiling water, and let it remain till the fruit is well done. Slices of bread, or boiled rice, may either be stewed with the fruit, or added when eaten.

FRUIT PASTE. Put any kind of fruit into a preserving pan, stir it till it will mash quite soft, and strain it. To one pint of juice, add a pound and a half of fine sugar; dissolve the sugar in water, and boil it till the water is dried up. Then mix it with the juice, boil it once, pour it into plates, and dry it in a stove. When wanted for use, cut it in strips, and make paste knots for garnishing.

FRUIT PUDDINGS. Make up a thick batter of milk and eggs, with a little flour and salt; put in any kind of fruit, and either bake or boil it. Apples should be pared and quartered, gooseberries and currants should be picked and cleaned, before they are put into the batter. Or make a thick paste, roll it out, and line a bason with it, after it has been rubbed with a little butter. Then fill it with fruit, put on a lid, tie it up close in a cloth, and boil it for two hours. The pudding will be lighter, if only made in a bason, then turned out into a pudding cloth, and boiled in plenty of water.

FRUIT STAINS. If stains of fruit or wine have been long in the linen, rub the part on each side with yellow soap. Then lay on a thick mixture of starch in cold water, rub it well in, and expose the linen to the sun and air till the stain comes out. If not removed in three or four days, rub off the mixture, and renew the process. When dry, it may be sprinkled with a little water.—Many other stains may be taken out by only dipping the linen into sour buttermilk, and drying it in a hot sun. Then wash it in cold water and dry it, two or three times a day.

FRUIT FOR TARTS. To preserve fruit for family desserts, whether cherries, plums, or apples, gather them when ripe, and put them in small jars that will hold about a pound. Strew over each jar six ounces of fine pounded sugar, and cover each with two bladders, separately tied down. Set the jars in a large stewpan of water up to the neck, and let it boil three hours gently. Keep these and all other sorts of fruit free from damp.

FRUIT TREES. When they have the appearance of being old or worn out, and are covered with moss and insects, they may be revived and made fruitful by dressing them well with a brush, dipped in a solution of strong fresh lime. The outer rind, with all its incumbrance, will then fall off; a new and clean one will be formed, and the trees put on a healthy appearance.

FRUITS IN JELLY. Put half a pint of calf's foot jelly into a bowl; when stiff, lay in three peaches, and a bunch of grapes with the stalk upwards. Cover over with vine leaves, and fill up the bowl with jelly. Let it stand till the next day, and then set it to the brim in hot water. When it gives way from the bowl, turn the jelly out carefully, and send it to table. Any kind of fruit may be treated in the same way.

FUEL. Coals constitute a principal article of domestic convenience, especially during the severity of winter. At that season they often become very scarce, and are sold at an extravagant price. To remedy this evil in some measure, take two-thirds of soft clay, free from stones, and work it into three or four bushels of small coals previously sifted: form this composition into balls or cakes, about three or four inches thick, and let them be thoroughly dried. When the fire burns clear, place four or five of these cakes in the front of the grate, where they will soon become red, and yield a clear and strong heat till they are totally consumed. The expense of a ton of this composition is but trifling, when compared with that of a chaldron of coals, as it may be prepared at one-fourth of the cost, and will be of greater service than a chaldron and a half of the latter. Coal dust worked up with horse dung, cow dung, saw dust, tanner's waste, or any other combustible matter that is not too expensive, will also be found a saving in the article of fuel. Nearly a third of the coals consumed in large towns and cities might be saved, if the coal ashes were preserved, instead of being thrown into the dust bins, and afterwards mixed with an equal quantity of small coal, moistened with water. This mixture thrown behind the fire, with a few round coals in front, would save the trouble of sifting the ashes, and make a cheerful and pleasant fire.——THE BEST MODE OF LIGHTING A FIRE.—Fill the grate with fresh coals quite up to the upper bar but one; then lay on the wood in the usual manner, rather collected in a mass than scattered. Over the wood place the cinders of the preceding day, piled up as high as the grate will admit, and placed loosely in rather large fragments, in order that the draft may be free: a bit or two of fresh coal may be added to the cinders when once they are lighted, but no small coal must be thrown on at first. When all is prepared, light the wood, when the cinders in a short time being thoroughly ignited, the gas rising from the coals below, which will now be affected by the heat, will take fire as it passes through them, leaving a very small portion of smoke to go up the chimney. One of the advantages of this mode of lighting a fire is, that small coal is better suited to the purpose than large, except a few pieces in front to keep the small from falling out of the grate. A fire lighted in this way will burn all day, without any thing being done to it. When apparently quite out, on being stirred, you have in a few minutes a glowing fire. When the upper part begins to cake, it must be stirred, but the lower must not be touched.

FUMIGATION. To prevent infection from fever, take a handful each of rue, sage, mint, rosemary, and lavender, all fresh gathered. Cut them small, put them into a stone jar, pour on a pint of the best white-wine vinegar, cover the jar close, and let it stand eight days in the sun, or near the fire. Then strain it off, and dissolve in it an ounce of camphor. This liquid sprinkled about the chamber, or fumigated, will much revive the patient, and prevent the attendants from receiving the infection. Or mix a spoonful of salt in a cup, with a little powdered magnesia: pour on the mixture at different times a spoonful of strong vitriolic acid, and the vapour arising from it will destroy the putrid effluvia.

FURNITURE LININGS. These articles require to be first washed, and afterwards dyed of a different colour, in order to change and improve their appearance.—For a Buff or salmon colour, according to the depth of the hue, rub down on a pewter plate two pennyworth of Spanish arnatto, and then boil it in a pail of water a quarter of an hour. Put into it two ounces of potash, stir it round, and instantly put in the lining. Stir it all the time it is boiling, which must be five or six minutes; then put it into cold spring water, and hang the articles up singly without wringing. When almost dry, fold the lining, and mangle it.—For Pink, the calico must be washed extremely clean, and thoroughly dried. Then boil it in two gallons of soft water, and four ounces of alum; take it out, and dry it in the air. Meanwhile boil in the alum water two handfuls of wheat bran till quite slippery, and then strain it. Take two scruples of cochineal, and two ounces of argall finely pounded and sifted, and mix it with the liquor a little at a time. Put the calico into the liquor, keep it stirring and boiling, till the liquor is nearly wasted. Then take out the calico, wash it first in chamber lye, and afterwards in cold water. Rinse it in water-starch strained, dry it quick without hanging it in folds, and let it be well mangled. It would be better still to have it callendered.—Blue. The calico must be washed clean and dried. Then mix some of Scott's liquid blue in as much water as will be sufficient to cover the things to be dyed, and add some starch to give it a light stiffness. Dry a small piece of the lining to see whether the colour is deep enough; and if approved, put it in and wash it in the dye. Dry the articles singly, and mangle or callender them.

FURS. To preserve them from the moth, comb them occasionally while in use. When not wanted, mix among them bitter apples from the druggists, in small muslin bags, sewing them in several folds of linen, carefully turned in at the edges. Keep the furs in a cool place, free from damp.

G.

GAD FLY. Cows and oxen are often so distressed by the darts of the gad fly, that they rush into the water for refuge till night approaches. The only remedy is to wash the backs of the cattle in the spring with strong tobacco-water, which would greatly prevent the generating of these vermin. When sheep are struck with the fly, the way is to clip off the wool, to rub the parts affected with powdered lime or wood ashes, and afterwards to anoint them with currier's oil, which will heal the wounds, and secure the animals from future attack. Or dissolve half an ounce of corrosive sublimate in two quarts of soft water, and add a quarter of a pint of spirits of turpentine. Cut off the wool as far as it is infected, pour a few drops of the mixture in a circle round the maggots produced by the flies, and afterwards rub a little of it among them, and the maggots will immediately be destroyed.

GAME. Game ought not to be thrown away even after it has been kept a long time, for when it seems to be spoiled it may often be made fit for eating, by carefully cleaning and washing it with vinegar and water. If there is danger of birds not keeping, the best way is to crop and draw them. Pick them clean, wash them in two or three waters, and rub them with salt. Plunge them into a kettle of boiling water one by one, and draw them up and down by the legs, that the water may pass through them. Let them remain in the water five or six minutes, and then hang them up in a cool place. When drained, season the insides well with pepper and salt, and wash them before they are roasted. The most delicate birds, even grouse, may thus be preserved. Those that live by suction cannot be done this way, as they are never drawn; and perhaps the heat might make them worse, as the water could not pass through them; but they will bear a high flavour. Lumps of charcoal put about birds and meat will preserve them from taint, and restore what is spoiling.

GAME SAUCE. Wash and pare a head of celery, cut it into thin slices, boil it gently till it becomes tender; then add a little beaten mace, pepper, salt, and nutmeg. Thicken it with flour and butter, boil it up, pour some of it in the dish, and some in a boat. Lemon pickle or lemon juice may be added to it.

GAMMON. Take off the rind of the ham and gammon, and soak it in water; cover the fat part with writing paper, roast, and baste it with canary. When done, sprinkle it over with crumbs of bread and parsley. Serve it with brown gravy, after it is well browned, and garnish it with raspings of bread.

GARDEN HEDGES. A well trained hawthorn fence is the strongest, but as it is apt to get thin and full of gaps at the bottom, the barberry is to be preferred, especially on high banks with a light soil. It may be raised from the berries as easily as hawthorn, and will grow faster, if the suckers be planted early. The barberry puts up numerous suckers from the roots; it will therefore always grow close at the bottom, and make an impenetrable fence. In trimming any kind of close hedge, care should be taken to slope the sides, and make it pointed at the top: otherwise, the bottom being shaded by the upper part, will make it grow thin and full of gaps. The sides of a young hedge may be trimmed, to make it bush the better; but it should not be topped till it has arrived at a full yard in height, though a few of the points may be taken off. The bottom of hawthorn hedges may be conveniently thickened, by putting in some plants of common sweet briar, or barberry.

GARDEN RHUBARB. To cultivate the common garden rhubarb, it should not only have a depth of good soil, but it should be watered in dry weather, and well covered with straw or dung in the winter season. It will then become solid when taken out of the ground; and if cut into large slices, and hung up in a warm kitchen, it will soon be fit for use. The plants may be taken up when the leaves are decayed, either in spring or in autumn, while the weather is dry; and when the roots are cleared from dirt, without washing, they should be dried in the sun for a few days before they are hung up. The better way would be to wrap them up separately in whited brown paper, and dry them on the hob of a common stove. Lemon and orange peel will dry remarkably well in the same manner.

GARGLES. Common gargles may be made of figs boiled in milk and water, with a little sal-ammoniac; or sage-tea, with honey and vinegar mixed together. A sore throat may be gargled with it two or three times a day.

GEESE. The rearing of this species of poultry incurs but little expense, as they chiefly support themselves on commons or in lanes, where they can get at water. The largest are esteemed the best, as also are the white and the grey: the pied and dark coloured are not so good. Thirty days are generally the time that the goose sets, but in warm weather she will sometimes hatch sooner. Give them plenty of food, such as scalded bran and light oats. As soon as the goslings are hatched, keep them housed for eight or ten days, and feed them with barley meal, bran, and curds. Green geese should begin to fatten at six or seven weeks old, and be fed as above. Stubble geese require no fattening, if they have the run of good fields and pasture.—If geese are bought at market, for the purpose of cooking, be careful to see that they are fresh and young. If fresh, the feet will be pliable: if stale, dry and stiff. The bill and feet of a young one will be yellow, and there will be but few hairs upon them: if old, they will be red. Green geese, not more than three or four months old, should be scalded: a stubble goose should be picked dry.

GEORGE PUDDING. Boil very tender a handful of whole rice in a small quantity of milk, with a large piece of lemon peel. Let it drain; then mix with it a dozen apples, boiled to a pulp as dry as possible. Add a glass of white wine, the yolks of five eggs, two ounces of orange and citron cut thin, and sweeten it with sugar. Line a mould or bason with a very good paste, beat the five whites of the eggs to a very strong froth, and mix it with the other ingredients. Fill the mould, and bake it of a fine brown colour. Serve it bottom upwards with the following sauce: two glasses of wine, a spoonful of sugar, the yolks of two eggs, and a piece of sugar the size of a walnut. Simmer without boiling, and pour to and from the saucepan till the sauce is of a proper thickness, and then put it in the dish.

GERMAN PUDDINGS. Melt three ounces of butter in a pint of cream, and let it stand till nearly cold. Then mix two ounces of fine flour, and two ounces of sugar, four yolks and two whites of eggs, and a little rose or orange flower water. Bake in little buttered cups half an hour. They should be served the moment they are done, and only when going to be eaten, or they will not be light. Turn the puffs out of the cups, and serve with white wine and sugar.

GERMAN PUFFS. Mix together two ounces of blanched almonds well beaten, a spoonful of rose water, one white and two yolks of eggs, a spoonful of flour, half a pint of cream, two ounces of butter, and sugar to taste. Butter some cups, half fill them, and put them in the oven. Serve with white wine sauce, butter, and sugar. This is esteemed a good middle dish for dinner or supper.

GIBLETS. Let the giblets be picked clean and washed, the feet skinned, the bill cut off, the head split in two, the pinion bones broken, the liver and gizzard cut in four, and the neck in two pieces. Put them into a pint of water, with pepper and salt, an onion, and sweet herbs. Cover the saucepan close, and stew them on a slow fire till they are quite tender. Take out the onion and herbs, and put them into a dish with the liquor.

GIBLET PIE. Clean and skin the giblets very carefully, stew them with a small quantity of water, onion, black pepper, and a bunch of sweet herbs, till nearly done. Let them grow cold: and if not enough to fill the dish, lay at the bottom two or three slices of veal, beef, or mutton. Add the liquor of the stew; and when the pie is baked, pour into it a large teacupful of cream. Sliced apples added to the pie are a great improvement. Duck giblets will do; but goose giblets are much to be preferred.

GIBLET SOUP. Scald and clean three or four sets of goose or duck giblets, and stew them slowly with a pound or two of gravy beef, scrag of mutton, or the bone of a knuckle of veal, an ox tail, or some shanks of mutton. Add a large bunch of sweet herbs, a tea-spoonful of white pepper, a large spoonful of salt, and three onions. Put in five pints of water, cut each of the gizzards into four pieces, and simmer till they become quite tender. Skin the stew carefully, add a quarter of a pint of cream, two tea-spoonfuls of mushroom powder, and an ounce of butter mixed with a dessert-spoonful of flour. Let it boil a few minutes, then put it into a tureen, add a little salt, and serve up the soup with the giblets. Instead of cream, it may be seasoned with a large spoonful of ketchup, some cayenne, and two glasses of sherry.

GILDED FRAMES. These valuable articles cannot be preserved from fly stains, without covering them with strips of paper, and suffering them to remain till the flies are gone. Previous to this, the light dust should be blown from the gilding, and a feather or a clean brush lightly passed over it.

Linen takes off the gilding, and deadens its brightness; it should therefore never be used for wiping it. Some means should be used to destroy the flies, as they injure furniture of every kind, and the paper likewise. Bottles hung about with sugar and vinegar, or beer, will attract them; or fly water, put into little shells placed about the room, but out of the reach of children.

GILLIFLOWER WINE. To three gallons of water put six pounds of the best raw sugar; boil the sugar and water together for the space of half an hour, and keep skimming it as the scum rises. Let it stand to cool, beat up three ounces of syrup of betony with a large spoonful of ale yeast, and put it into the liquor. Prepare a peck of gilliflowers, cut from the stalks, and put them in to infuse and work together for three days, the whole being covered with a cloth. Strain it, and put it into a cask; let it settle for three or four weeks, and then bottle it.

GINGER BEER. To every gallon of spring water add one ounce of sliced white ginger, one pound of lump sugar, and two ounces of lemon juice. Boil the mixture nearly an hour, and take off the scum; then run it through a hair sieve into a tub, and when cool, add yeast in the proportion of half a pint to nine gallons. Keep it in a temperate situation two days, during which it may be stirred six or eight times. Then put it into a cask, which must be kept full, and the yeast taken off at the bunghole with a spoon. In a fortnight, add half a pint of fining to nine gallons of the liquor, which will clear it by ascent, if it has been properly fermented. The cask must still be kept full, and the rising particles taken off at the bunghole. When fine, which may be expected in twenty-four hours, bottle and cork it well; and in summer it will be ripe and fit to drink in a fortnight.

GINGER DROPS. Beat two ounces of fresh candied orange in a mortar, with a little sugar, till reduced to a paste. Then mix an ounce of the powder of white ginger, with a pound of loaf sugar. Wet the sugar with a little water, and boil all together to a candy, and drop it on white paper the size of mint drops. These make an excellent stomachic.

GINGER WINE. To seven gallons of water put nineteen pounds of moist sugar, and boil it for half an hour, taking off the scum as it rises. Then take a small quantity of the liquor, and add to it nine ounces of the best ginger bruised. Put it all together, and when nearly cold, chop nine pounds of raisins very small, and put them into a nine gallon cask, with one ounce of isinglass. Slice four lemons into the cask, taking out all the seeds, and pour the liquor over them, with half a pint of fresh yeast. Leave it unstopped for three weeks, and in about three months it will be fit for bottling. There will be one gallon of the sugar and water more than the cask will hold at first: this must be kept to fill up as the liquor works off, as it is necessary that the cask should be kept full, til it has done working. The raisins should be two thirds Malaga, and one third Muscadel. Spring and autumn are the best seasons for making this wine.—Another. Boil nine quarts of water with six pounds of lump sugar, the rinds of two or three lemons very thinly pared, and two ounces of bruised white ginger. Let it boil half an hour, and skim it well. Put three quarters of a pound of raisins into the cask; and when the liquor is lukewarm, turn it, adding the juice of two lemons strained, with a spoonful and a half of yeast. Stir it daily, then put in half a pint of brandy, and half an ounce of isinglass shavings. Stop it up, and bottle it in six or seven weeks. The lemon peel is not to be put into the barrel.

GINGERBREAD. Mix with two pounds of flour, half a pound of treacle, and half a pound of butter, adding an ounce of ginger finely powdered and sifted, and three quarters of an ounce of caraway seeds. Having worked it very much, set it to rise before the fire. Then roll out the paste, cut it into any shape, and bake it on tins. If to be made into sweetmeats, add some candied orange-peel, shred into small pieces.—Another sort. To three quarters of a pound of treacle, put one egg beaten and strained. Mix together four ounces of brown sugar, half an ounce of sifted ginger, and a quarter of an ounce each of cloves, mace, allspice, and nutmeg, beaten as fine as possible; also a quarter of an ounce of coriander and caraway seeds. Melt a pound of butter, and mix with the above, adding as much flour as will knead it into a pretty stiff paste. Roll it out, cut it into cakes, bake them on tin plates in a quick oven, and a little time will do them. Gingerbread buttons or drops may be made of a part of the paste.—A plain sort of gingerbread may be prepared as follows. Mix three pounds of flour with half a pound of butter, four ounces of brown sugar, and half an ounce of pounded ginger. Make it into a paste, with a pound and a quarter of warm treacle. Or make the gingerbread without butter, by mixing two pounds of treacle with the following ingredients. Four ounces each of orange, lemon, citron, and candied ginger, all thinly sliced; one ounce each of coriander seeds, caraways, and pounded ginger, adding as much flour as will make it into a soft paste. Lay it in cakes on tin plates, and bake it in a quick oven. Keep it dry in a covered earthen vessel, and the gingerbread will be good for some months. If cakes or biscuits be kept in paper, or a drawer, the taste will be disagreeable. A tureen, or a pan and cover, will preserve them long and moist; or if intended to be crisp, laying them before the fire, or keeping them in a dry canister, will make them so.

GINGERBREAD NUTS. Carefully melt half a pound of butter, and stir it up in two pounds of treacle. Add an ounce of pounded ginger, two ounces of preserved lemon and orange peel, two ounces of preserved angelica cut small, one of coriander seed pounded, and the same of caraway whole. Mix them together, with two eggs, and as much flour as will bring it to a fine paste. Make it into nuts, put them on a tin plate, and bake them in a quick oven.

GLASS. Broken glass may be mended with the same cement as china, or if it be only cracked, it will be sufficient to moisten the part with the white of an egg, strewing it over with a little powdered lime, and instantly applying a piece of fine linen. Another cement for glass is prepared from two parts of litharge, one of quick lime, and one of flint glass, each separately and finely powdered, and the whole worked up into a paste with drying oil. This compound is very durable, and acquires a greater degree of hardness when immersed in water.

GLASSES. These frail and expensive articles may be rendered less brittle, and better able to bear sudden changes of temperature, by first plunging them into cold water, then gradually heating the water till it boils, and suffering it to cool in the open air. Glasses of every description, used for the table, will afterwards bear boiling water suddenly poured into them, without breaking. When they have been tarnished by age or accident, their lustre may be restored by strewing on them some fuller's earth, carefully powdered and cleared of sand and dirt, and then rubbing them gently with a linen cloth, or a little putty.

GLOVES. Leather gloves may be repaired, cleaned, and dyed of a fine yellow, by steeping a little saffron in boiling water for about twelve hours; and having lightly sewed up the tops of the gloves, to prevent the dye from staining the insides, wet them over with a sponge or soft brush dipped in the liquid. A teacupful will be sufficient for a single pair.

GLOUCESTER CHEESE. This article is made of milk immediately from the cow; and if it be too hot in the summer, a little skim milk or water is added to it, before the rennet is put in. As soon as the curd is come it is broken small, and cleared of the whey. The curd is set in the press for about a quarter of an hour, in order to extract the remainder of the liquid. It is then put into the cheese tub again, broken small, and scalded with water mixed with a little whey. When the curd is settled, the liquor is poured off; the curd is put into a vat, and worked up with a little salt when about half full. The vat is then filled up, and the whole is turned two or three times in it, the edges being pared, and the middle rounded up at each turning. At length, the curd being put into a cloth, it is placed in the press, then laid on the shelves, and turned every day till it becomes sufficiently firm to bear washing.

GLOUCESTER JELLY. Take rice, sago, pearl barley, hartshorn shavings, and eringo root, each one ounce. Simmer with three pints of water till reduced to one, and then strain it. When cold it will be a jelly; of which give, dissolved in wine, milk, or broth, in change with other nourishment.

GNATS. The stings of these troublesome insects are generally attended with a painful swelling. One of the most effectual remedies consists of an equal mixture of turpentine and sweet oil, which should immediately be applied to the wounded part, and it will afford relief in a little time. Olive oil alone, unsalted butter, or fresh lard, if rubbed on without delay, will also be found to answer the same purpose. They may be destroyed by fumigation, the same as for flies.

GOLD. To clean gold, and restore its lustre, dissolve a little sal ammoniac in common wine. Boil the gold in it, and it will soon recover its brilliance. To clean gold or silver lace, sew it up in a linen cloth, and boil it with two ounces of soap in a pint of water: afterwards wash the lace in clear water. When the lace happens to be tarnished, the best liquor for restoring its lustre is spirits of wine, which should be warmed before it is applied. This application will also preserve the colour of silk or embroidery.

GOLD RINGS. If a ring sticks tight on the finger, and cannot easily be removed, touch it with mercury, and it will become so brittle that a slight blow will break it.

GOOSE FEATHERS. These being deemed particularly valuable, the birds in some counties are plucked four or five times in a year. The first operation is performed in the spring for feathers and quills, and is repeated for feathers only, between that period and Michaelmas. Though the plucking of geese appears to be a barbarous custom, yet experience has proved, that if carefully done, the birds thrive better, and are more healthy, when stripped of their feathers, than if they were left to drop them by moulting. Geese intended for breeding in farm yards, and which are called old geese, may be plucked three times a year, at an interval of seven weeks, but not oftener. Every one should be thirteen or fourteen weeks old before they are subject to this operation, or they are liable to perish in cold summers; and if intended for the table, they would become poor and lose their quality, were they stripped of their feathers at an earlier period.

GOOSE PIE. Quarter a goose, season it well, put it in a baking dish, and lay pieces of butter over it. Put on a raised crust, and bake it in a moderate oven. To make a richer pie, forcemeat may be added, and slices of tongue. Duck pie is made in the same manner.

GOOSE SAUCE. Put into melted butter a spoonful of sorrel juice, a little sugar, and some scalded gooseberries. Pour it into boats, and send it hot to table.

GOOSEBERRY FOOL. Put the fruit into a stone jar, with some good Lisbon sugar. Set the jar on a stove, or in a saucepan of water over the fire: if the former, a large spoonful of water should be added to the fruit. When it is done enough to pulp, press it through a cullender. Have ready a sufficient quantity of new milk, and a tea-cupful of raw cream, boiled together, or an egg instead of the latter. When cold, sweeten it pretty well with fine Lisbon sugar, and mix the pulp with it by degrees.

GOOSEBERRY HOPS. Gather the largest green gooseberries of the walnut kind, and slit the tops into four quarters, leaving the stalk end whole. Pick out the seeds, and with a strong needle and thread fasten five or six together, by running the thread through the bottoms, till they are of the size of a hop. Lay vine leaves at the bottom of a tin preserving-pan, cover them with the hops, then a layer of leaves, and so on: lay a good many on the top, and fill the pan with water. Stop it down so close that no steam can escape, set it by a slow fire till scalding hot, and then take it off to cool. Repeat the operation till the gooseberries, on being opened, are found to be of a good green. Then drain them on sieves, and make a thin syrup of a pound of sugar to a pint of water, well boiled and skimmed. When the syrup is half cold, put in the fruit; give it a boil up, and repeat it thrice. Gooseberry hops look well and eat best dried, and in this case they may be set to dry in a week. But if to be kept moist, make a syrup in the above proportions, adding a slice of ginger in the boiling. When skimmed and clear, give the gooseberries one boil, and pour the syrup cold over them. If found too sour, a little sugar may be added, before the hops that are for drying receive their last boil. The extra syrup will serve for pies, or go towards other sweetmeats.

GOOSEBERRY JAM. Gather some ripe gooseberries, of the clear white or green sort, pick them clean and weigh them. Allow three quarters of a pound of lump sugar to a pound of fruit, and half a pint of water. Boil and skim the sugar and water, then put in the fruit, and boil it gently till it is quite clear. Break the gooseberries into jam, and put into small pots.—Another. Gather some ripe gooseberries in dry weather, of the red hairy sort, and pick off the heads and tails. Put twelve pounds of them into a preserving pan, with a pint of currant juice, drawn as for jelly. Boil them pretty quick, and beat them with a spoon; when they begin to break, add six pounds of white Lisbon sugar, and simmer them slowly to a jam. They require long boiling, or they will not keep; but they make an excellent jam for tarts and puffs. When the jam is put into jars, examine it after two or three days; and if the syrup and fruit separate, the whole must be boiled again. In making white gooseberry jam, clarified sugar should be used; and in all cases great care must be taken to prevent the fruit from burning to the bottom of the pan.

GOOSEBERRY PUDDING. Stew some gooseberries in a jar over a hot hearth, or in a saucepan of water, till reduced to a pulp. Take a pint of the juice pressed through a coarse sieve, and mix it with three eggs beaten and strained. Add an ounce and a half of butter, sweeten it well, put a crust round the dish, and bake it. A few crumbs of roll should be mixed with the above to give it a little consistence, or four ounces of Naples biscuits.

GOOSEBERRY TRIFLE. Scald as much fruit as when pulped through a sieve, will cover the bottom of a dish intended to be used. Mix with it the rind of half a lemon grated fine, sweetened with sugar. Put any quantity of common custard over it, and a whip on the top, as for other trifles.

GOOSEBERRY VINEGAR. Boil some spring water; and when cold, put to every three quarts, a quart of bruised gooseberries in a large tub. Let them remain two or three days, stirring often; then strain through a hair bag, and to each gallon of liquor add a pound of the coarsest sugar. Put it into a barrel, with yeast spread upon a toast, and cover the bung hole with a piece of slate. The greater the quantity of sugar and fruit, the stronger the vinegar.

GOOSEBERRY WINE. When the weather is dry, gather gooseberries about the time they are half ripe. Pick them clean as much as a peck into a convenient vessel, and bruise them with a piece of wood, taking as much care as possible to keep the seeds whole. Now having put the pulp into a canvas bag, press out all the juice; and to every gallon of the gooseberries, add about three pounds of fine loaf sugar. Mix the whole together by stirring it with a stick, and as soon as the sugar is quite dissolved, pour it into a cask which will exactly hold it. If the quantity be about eight or nine gallons, let it stand a fortnight: if twenty gallons, forty days, and so on in proportion. Set it in a cool place; and after standing the proper time, draw it off from the lees. Put it into another clean vessel of equal size, or into the same, after pouring out the lees and making it clean. Let a cask of ten or twelve gallons stand for about three months, and twenty gallons for five months, after which it will be fit for bottling off.

GOOSEBERRIES PRESERVED. Gather some dry gooseberries of the hairy sort, before the seeds become large, and take care not to cut them in taking off the stalks and buds. If gathered in the damp, or the gooseberry skins are the least broken in the preparation, the fruit will mould. Fill some jars or wide-mouthed bottles, put the corks loosely in, and set the bottles up to the neck in a kettle of water. When the fruit looks scalded, take them out; and when perfectly cold, cork them down close, and rosin the top. Dig a trench sufficiently deep to receive all the bottles, and cover them with the earth a foot and a half. When a frost comes on, a little fresh litter from the stable will prevent the ground from hardening, so that the fruit may more easily be dug up.—Green gooseberries may also be preserved for winter use, without bedding them in the earth. Scald them as above, and when cold, fill the bottles up with cold water. Cork and rosin them down, and keep them in a dry place.—Another way. Having prepared the gooseberries as above, prepare a kettle of boiling water, and put into it as much roche alum as will harden the water, or give it a little roughness when dissolved: but if there be too much it will spoil the fruit. Cover the bottom of a large sieve with gooseberries, without laying one upon another; and hold the sieve in the water till the fruit begins to look scalded on the outside. Turn them gently out of the sieve on a cloth on the dresser, cover them with another cloth, putting some more to be scalded, till the whole are finished. Observe not to put one quantity upon another, or they will become too soft. The next day pick out any bad or broken ones, bottle the rest, and fill up the bottles with the alum water in which they were scalded. If the water be left in the kettle, or in a glazed pan, it will spoil; it must therefore be quickly put into the bottles. Gooseberries prepared in this way, and stopped down close, will make as fine tarts as when fresh from the trees.—Another way. In dry weather pick some full grown but unripe gooseberries, top and tail them, and put them into wide-mouthed bottles. Stop them lightly with new velvet corks, put them into the oven after the bread is drawn, and let them stand till they are shrunk one fourth. Take them out of the oven, fasten the corks in tight, cut off the tops, and rosin them down close. Set them in a dry place; and if well secured from the air, they will keep the year round. Currants and damsons may be preserved in the same way.

GOOSEGRASS OINTMENT. Melt some hog's lard, add as much clivers or goosegrass as the lard will moisten, and boil them together over a slow fire. Keep the mixture stirring till it becomes a little brown, and then strain it through a cloth. When cold, take the ointment from the water, and put it up in gallipots.

GOUT. Gouty patients are required to abstain from all fermented and spirituous liquors, and to use wine very moderately; carefully to avoid all fat, rancid, and salted provisions, and high seasoned dishes of every description. The constant use of barley bread is recommended, with large doses of powdered ginger boiled in milk for breakfast. Absorbent powders of two scruples of magnesia, and three or four grains each of rhubarb and purified kali, should be taken during the intervals of gouty fits, and repeated every other morning for several weeks. The feet should be kept warm, sinapisms frequently applied to them, and the part affected should be covered with flannel.

GOUT CORDIAL. Take four pounds of sun raisins sliced and stoned, two ounces of senna, one ounce of fennel seed, one of coriander, half an ounce of cochineal, half an ounce of saffron, half an ounce of stick liquorice, and half a pound of rhubarb: infuse them all in two gallons of brandy, and let it stand for ten days. Stir it occasionally, then strain it off, and bottle it. Take a small wine-glass full, when the gout is in the head or stomach; and if the pain be not removed, take two large spoonfuls more.— Or take six drams of opium, half an ounce of soap of tartar, half an ounce of castile soap, one dram of grated nutmeg, three drams of camphor, two scruples of saffron, and nine ounces of sweet spirit of sal-ammoniac. Put them all into a wine flask in a sand-heat for ten days, shaking it occasionally till the last day or two: then pour it off clear, and keep it stopped up close for use. Take thirty or forty drops in a glass of peppermint two hours after eating; it may also be taken two or three times in the day or night if required.

GRANARIES. These depositaries are very liable to be infested with weasels, and various kinds of insects. To prevent their depredations, the floors of granaries should be laid with poplars of Lombardy.

GRAPES. To preserve this valuable fruit, prepare a cask or barrel, by carefully closing up its crevices to prevent access of the external air. Place a layer of bran, which has been well dried in an oven; upon this place a layer of bunches of grapes, well cleaned, and gathered in the afternoon of a dry day, before they are perfectly ripe. Proceed then with alternate layers of bran and grapes till the barrel is full, taking care that the bunches of grapes do not touch each other, and to let the last layer be of bran; then close the barrel so that the air may not be able to penetrate. Grapes thus packed will keep for a twelvemonth. To restore their freshness, cut the end of each bunch, and put that of white grapes into white wine, and that of black grapes into red wine, as flowers are put into water to keep them fresh. It is customary in France to pack grapes for the London market in saw dust, but it must be carefully dried with a gentle heat, or the turpentine and other odours of the wood will not fail to injure the fruit. Oak saw dust will answer the purpose best.

GRAPE WINE. To every gallon of ripe grapes put a gallon of soft water, bruise the grapes, let them stand a week without stirring, and draw the liquor off fine. To every gallon of liquor allow three pounds of lump sugar, put the whole into a vessel, but do not stop it till it has done hissing; then stop it close, and in six months it will be fit for bottling.—A better wine, though smaller in quantity, will be made by leaving out the water, and diminishing the quantity of sugar. Water is necessary only where the juice is so scanty, or so thick, as in cowslip, balm, or black currant wine, that it could not be used without it.

GRAVEL. The gout or rheumatism has a tendency to produce this disorder; it is also promoted by the use of sour liquor, indigestible food, especially cheese, and by a sedentary life. Perspiration should be assisted by gentle means, particularly by rubbing with a warm flannel; the diet regulated by the strictest temperance, and moderate exercise is not to be neglected. For medicine, take the juice of a horseradish, made into a thin syrup by mixing it with sugar; a spoonful or two to be taken every three or four hours.

GRAVEL WALKS. To preserve garden walks from moss and weeds, water them frequently with brine, or salt and water, both in the spring and in autumn. Worms may be destroyed by an infusion of walnut-tree leaves, or by pouring into the holes a ley made of wood ashes and lime. If fruit trees are sprinkled with it, the ravages of insects will be greatly prevented.

GRAVIES. A few general observations are necessary on the subject of soups and gravies. When there is any fear of gravy meat being spoiled before it be wanted, it should be well seasoned, and lightly fried, in order to its keeping a day or two longer; but the gravy is best when the juices are fresh. When soups or gravies are to be put by, let them be changed every day into fresh scalded pans. Whatever liquor has vegetables boiled in it, is apt to turn sour much sooner than the juices of meat, and gravy should never be kept in any kind of metal. When fat remains on any soup, a teacupful of flour and water mixed quite smooth, and boiled in, will take it off.

If richness or greater consistence be required, a good lump of butter mixed with flour, and boiled in the soup or gravy, will impart either of these qualities. Long boiling is necessary to obtain the full flavour; and gravies and soups are best made the day before they are wanted. They are also much better when the meat is laid in the bottom of the pan, and stewed with herbs, roots, and butter, than when water is put to the meat at first; and the gravy that is drawn from the meat, should almost be dried up before the water is added. The sediment of gravies that have stood to be cold, should not be used in cooking. When onions are strong, boil a turnip with them, if for sauce; and this will make them mild and pleasant. If soups or gravies are too weak, do not cover them in boiling, that the watery particles may evaporate. A clear jelly of cow heels is very useful to keep in the house, being a great improvement to soups and gravies. Truffles and morels thicken soups and sauces, and give them a fine flavour. The way is to wash half an ounce of each carefully, then simmer them a few minutes in water, and add them with the liquor to boil in the sauce till quite tender. As to the materials of which gravy is to be made, beef skirts will make as good as any other meat. Beef kidney, or milt, cut into small pieces, will answer the purpose very well; and so will the shank end of mutton that has been dressed, if much be wanted. The shank bones of mutton, if well soaked and cleaned, are a great improvement to the richness of the gravy. Taragon gives the flavour of French cookery, and in high gravies it is a great improvement; but it should be added only a short time before serving. To draw gravy that will keep for a week, cut some lean beef thin, put it into a fryingpan without any butter, cover it up, and set it on the fire, taking care that it does not burn. Keep it on the fire till all the gravy that comes out of the meat is absorbed, then add as much water as will cover the meat, and keep it stewing. Put in some herbs, onions, spice, and a piece of lean ham. Let it simmer till it is quite rich, and keep it in a cool place; but do not remove the fat till the gravy is to be used.

GRAVY FOR FOWL. When there is no meat to make gravy of, wash the feet of the fowl nicely, and cut them and the neck small. Simmer them with a little bread browned, a slice of onion, a sprig of parsley and thyme, some salt and pepper, and the liver and gizzard, in a quarter of a pint of water, till half wasted. Take out the liver, bruise it, and strain the liquor to it. Then thicken it with flour and butter, and a tea-spoonful of mushroom ketchup will make the gravy very good.

GRAVY FOR WILD FOWL. Set on a saucepan with half a pint of veal gravy, adding half a dozen leaves of basil, a small onion, and a roll of orange or lemon peel. Let it boil up for a few minutes, and strain it off. Put to the clear gravy the juice of a Seville orange, half a teaspoonful of salt, the same of pepper, and a glass of red wine. Shalot and cayenne may be added. This is an excellent sauce for all kinds of wild water-fowl, and should be sent up hot in a boat, as some persons like wild fowl very little done, and without any sauce. The common way of gashing the breast, and squeezing in a lemon, cools and hardens the flesh, and compels every one to eat it that way, whether they approve of it or not.

GRAVY FOR MUTTON. To make mutton taste like venison, provide for it the following gravy. Pick a very stale woodcock or snipe, and cut it to pieces, after having removed the bag from the entrails. Simmer it in some meat gravy, without seasoning; then strain it, and serve it with the mutton.

GRAVY SOUP. Wash and soak a leg of beef; break the bone, and set it on the fire with a gallon of water, a large bunch of sweet herbs, two large onions sliced and fried to a fine brown, but not burnt; add two blades of mace, three cloves, twenty berries of allspice, and forty black peppers. Stew the soup till it is rich, and then take out the meat, which may be eaten at the kitchen table, with a little of the gravy. Next day take off the fat, which will serve for basting, or for common pie crust. Slice some carrots, turnips, and celery, and simmer them till tender. If not approved, they can be taken out before the soup is sent to table, but the flavour will be a considerable addition. Boil vermicelli a quarter of an hour, and add to it a large spoonful of soy, and one of mushroom ketchup. A French roll should be made hot, then soaked in the soup, and served in the tureen.

GRAVY WITHOUT MEAT. Put into a bason a glass of small beer, a glass of water, some pepper and salt, grated lemon peel, a bruised clove or two, and a spoonful of walnut pickle, or mushroom ketchup. Slice an onion, flour and fry it in a piece of butter till it is brown. Then turn all the above into a small tosser, with the onion, and simmer it covered for twenty minutes. Strain it off for use, and when cold take off the fat.

GRAYLINE. Having scaled and washed the fish, then dry them. Dust them over with flour, and lay them separately on a board before the fire. Fry them of a fine colour with fresh dripping; serve them with crimp parsley, and plain butter. Perch and tench may be done the same way.

GREASE EXTRACTED. The ashes of burnt bones finely powdered, or calcined hartshorn, heated over the fire in a clean vessel, and laid on each side of the grease spot, if on books or paper, with a weight laid upon it to assist the effect, will completely remove it; or the powder may be wrapped in thin muslin, and applied in the same manner. When prints get foul and dirty, they may readily be cleaned in the same manner as linen is bleached, by being exposed to the sun and air, and frequently wetted with clean water. If this do not fully succeed, the print may be soaked in hot water; and if pasted on canvas, it should first be taken off by dipping it in boiling water, which will loosen it from the canvas. The dirt occasioned by flies, may be gently taken off with a wet sponge, after the print has been well soaked. Spots of white-wash may be removed by spirit of sea salt diluted with water.—If grease spots appear in leather, a different process must be pursued. A paste made of mealy potatoes, dry mustard, and spirits of turpentine, mixed together, and applied to the spot, will extract the grease from leather, if rubbed off after it has been allowed sufficient time to dry. A little vinegar may be added, to render the application more effectual.

GREEN FRUIT. Green peaches, plums, or other fruit, should be put into a preserving pan of spring water, covered with vine leaves, and set over a clear fire. When they begin to simmer take them off, and take the fruit out carefully with a slice. Peel and preserve them as other fruit.

GREEN GAGES. In order to preserve them for pies and tarts, choose the largest when they begin to soften. Split them without paring; and having weighed an equal quantity of sugar, strew a part of it over the fruit. Blanch the kernels with a small sharp knife. Next day pour the syrup from the fruit, and boil it gently six or eight minutes with the other sugar; skim it, and add the plums and kernels. Simmer it till clear, taking off any scum that rises; put the fruit singly into small pots, and pour the syrup and kernels to it. If the fruit is to be candied, the syrup must not be added: for the sake of variety, it may be proper to do some each way.

GREEN GOOSE PIE. Bone two young green geese, of a good size; but first take away every plug, and singe them nicely. Wash them clean, and season them well with salt, pepper, mace, and allspice. Put one inside the other, and press them quite close, drawing the legs inward. Put a good deal of butter over them, and bake them either with or without a crust: if the latter, a cover to the dish must fit close to keep in the steam.

GREEN PEAS. Peas should not be shelled till they are wanted, nor boiled in much water. Put them in when the water boils, with a little salt, and a lump of sugar. When they begin to dent in the middle, they are done enough. Strain them through a cullender, put a piece of butter in the dish, and stir them till it is melted. Garnish with boiled mint.

GREEN PEAS PRESERVED. If it be wished to keep them for winter use, shell the peas, and put them into a kettle of water when it boils. Warm them well, without boiling, and pour them into a cullender. When the water drains off, turn them out on a dresser covered with a cloth, and put over another cloth to dry them perfectly. Deposit them in wide-mouth bottles, leaving only room to pour clarified mutton suet upon them an inch thick, and also for the cork. Rosin it down, and keep it in the cellar or in the earth, the same as other green fruit. When the peas are to be used, boil them tender, with a piece of butter, a spoonful of sugar, and a little mint.— Another way. Shell the peas, scald and dry them as above. Put them on tins or earthen dishes in a cool oven once or twice to harden, and keep them in paper bags hung up in the kitchen. When they are to be used, let them be an hour in water; then set them on with cold water, a piece of butter, and a sprig of dried mint, and boil them.

GREEN PEAS SOUP. In shelling the peas, divide the old from the young. Stew the old ones to a pulp, with an ounce of butter, a pint of water, a leaf or two of lettuce, two onions, pepper and salt. Put to the liquor that stewed them some more water, the hearts and tender stalks of the lettuces, the young peas, a handful of spinach cut small, salt and pepper to relish, and boil them till quite soft. If the soup be too thin, or not rich enough, add an ounce or two of butter, mixed with a spoonful of rice or flour, and boil it half an hour longer. Before serving, boil in the soup some green mint shred fine. When the peas first come in, or are very young, the stock may be made of the shells washed and boiled, till they are capable of being pulped. More thickening will then be wanted.

GREEN PEAS STEWED. Put into a stewpan a quart of peas, a lettuce and an onion both sliced, and no more water than hangs about the lettuce from washing. Add a piece of butter, a little pepper and salt, and stew them very gently for two hours. When to be served, beat up an egg, and stir it into them, or a bit of flour and butter. Chop a little mint, and stew in them. Gravy may be added, or a tea-spoonful of white powdered sugar; but the flavour of the peas themselves is much better.

GREEN SAUCE. Mix a quarter of a pint of sorrel juice, a glass of white wine, and some scalded gooseberries. Add sugar, and a bit of butter, and boil them up, to serve with green geese or ducklings.

GRIDIRON. The bars of a gridiron should be made concave, and terminate in a trough to catch the gravy, and keep the fat from dropping into the fire and making a smoke, which will spoil the broiling. Upright gridirons are the best, as they can be used at any fire, without fear of smoke, and the gravy is preserved in the trough under them. The business of the gridiron may be done by a Dutch oven, when occasion requires.

GRIEF. In considering what is conducive to health or otherwise, it is impossible to overlook this destructive passion, which like envy is 'the rottenness of the bones.' Anger and fear are more violent, but this is more fixed: it sinks deep into the mind, and often proves fatal. It may generally be conquered at the beginning of any calamity; but when it has gained strength, all attempts to remove it are ineffectual. Life may be dragged out for a few years, but it is impossible that any one should enjoy health, whose mind is bowed down with grief and trouble. In this case some betake themselves to drinking, but here the remedy only aggravates the disease. The best relief, besides what the consolations of religion may afford, is to associate with the kind and cheerful, to shift the scene as much as possible, to keep up a succession of new ideas, apply to the study of some art or science, and to read and write on such subjects as deeply engage the attention. These will sooner expel grief than the most sprightly amusements, which only aggravate instead of relieving the anguish of a wounded heart.

GRILL SAUCE. To half a pint of gravy add an ounce of fresh butter, and a table-spoonful of flour, previously well rubbed together; the same of mushroom or walnut ketchup, two tea-spoonfuls of lemon juice, one of made mustard, one of caper, half a one of black pepper, a little lemon peel grated fine, a tea-spoonful of essence of anchovies, a very small piece of minced shalot, and a little chili vinegar, or a few grains of cayenne. Simmer them all together for a few minutes, pour a little of it over the grill, and send up the rest in a sauce tureen.

GRILLED MUTTON. Cut a breast of mutton into diamonds, rub it over with egg, and strew on some crumbs of bread and chopped parsley. Broil it in a Dutch oven, baste it with butter, and pour caper sauce or gravy into the dish.

GROUND RICE MILK. Boil one spoonful of ground rice, rubbed down smooth, with three half pints of milk, a little cinnamon, lemon peel, and nutmeg. Sweeten it when nearly done.

GROUND RICE PUDDING. Boil a large spoonful of ground rice in a pint of new milk, with lemon peel and cinnamon. When cold, add sugar, nutmeg, and two eggs well beaten. Bake it with a crust round the dish. A pudding of Russian seed is made in the same manner.

GROUSE. Twist the head under the wing, and roast them like fowls, but they must not be overdone. Serve with a rich gravy in the dish, and bread sauce. The sauce recommended for wild fowl, may be used instead of gravy.

GRUBS. Various kinds of grubs or maggots, hatched from beetles, are destructive of vegetation, and require to be exterminated. In a garden they may be taken and destroyed by cutting a turf, and laying it near the plant which is attacked, with the grass side downwards. But the most effectual way is to visit these depredators at midnight, when they may be easily found and destroyed.

GUDGEONS. These delicate fish are taken in running streams, where the water is clear. They come in about midsummer, and are to be had for five or six months. They require to be dressed much the same as smelts, being considered as a species of fresh-water smelts.

GUINEA FOWL. Pea and guinea fowl eat much like pheasants, and require to be dressed in the same way.

GUINEA HENS. These birds lay a great number of eggs; and if their nest can be discovered, it is best to put them under common hens, which are better nurses. They require great warmth, quiet, and careful feeding with rice swelled in milk, or bread soaked in it. Put two peppercorns down their throat when first hatched.

GUNPOWDER. Reduce to powder separately, five drams of nitrate of potass, one dram of sulphur, and one of new-burnt charcoal. Mix them together in a mortar with a little water, so as to make the compound into a dough, which roll out into round pieces of the thickness of a pin, upon a slab. This must be done by moving a board backwards and forwards until the dough is of a proper size. When three or four of these strings or pieces are ready, put them together, and with a knife cut the whole off in small grains. Place these grains on a sheet of paper in a warm place, and they will soon dry. During granulation, the dough must be prevented from sticking, by using a little of the dry compound powder. This mode of granulation, though tedious, is the only one to be used for so small a quantity, for the sake of experiment. In a large way, gunpowder is granulated by passing the composition through sieves.

H.

HADDOCKS. These fish may be had the greater part of the year, but are most in season during the first three months. In choosing, see that the flesh is firm, the eyes bright, and the gills fresh and red. Clean them well, dry them in a cloth, and rub them with vinegar to prevent the skin from breaking. Dredge them with flour, rub the gridiron with suet, and let it be hot when the fish is laid on. Turn them while broiling, and serve them up with melted butter, or shrimp sauce.

HAIR. Frequent cutting of the hair is highly beneficial to the whole body; and if the head be daily washed with cold water, rubbed dry, and exposed to the air, it will be found an excellent preventive of periodical headachs. Pomatums and general perfumery are very injurious; but a mixture of olive oil and spirits of rosemary, with a few drops of oil of nutmeg, may be used with safety. If a lead comb be sometimes passed through the hair, it will assume a darker colour, but for health it cannot be recommended.

HAIR POWDER. To know whether this article be adulterated with lime, as is too frequently the case, put a little of the powder of sal-ammoniac into it, and stir it up with warm water. If the hair powder has been adulterated with lime, a strong smell of alkali will arise from the mixture.

HAIR WATER. To thicken the hair, and prevent its falling off, an excellent water may be prepared in the following manner. Put four pounds of pure honey into a still, with twelve handfuls of the tendrils of vines, and the same quantity of rosemary tops. Distil as cool and as slowly as possible, and the liquor may be allowed to drop till it begins to taste sour.

HAMS. When a ham is to be dressed, put it into water all night, if it has hung long; and let it lie either in a hole dug in the earth, or on damp stones sprinkled with water, two or three days, to mellow it. Wash it well, and put it into a boiler with plenty of water; let it simmer four, five, or six hours, according to the size. When done enough, if before the time of serving, cover it with a clean cloth doubled, and keep the dish hot over some boiling water. Take off the skin, and rasp some bread over the ham. Preserve the skin as whole as possible, to cover the ham when cold, in order to prevent its drying. Garnish the dish with carrot when sent to table. If a dried ham is to be purchased, judge of its goodness by sticking a sharp knife under the bone. If it comes out with a pleasant smell, the ham is good: but if the knife be daubed, and has a bad scent, do not buy it. Hams short in the hock are best, and long-legged pigs are not fit to be pickled.

HAM SAUCE. When a ham is almost done with, pick all the meat clean from the bone, leaving out any rusty part. Beat the meat and the bone to a mash, put it into a saucepan with three spoonfuls of gravy, set it over a slow fire, and stir it all the time, or it will stick to the bottom. When it has been on some time, put to it a small bundle of sweet herbs, some pepper, and half a pint of beef gravy. Cover it up, and let it stew over a gentle fire. When it has a good flavour of the herbs, strain off the gravy. A little of this sauce will be found an improvement to all gravies.

HANDS. When the hands or feet are severely affected with the cold, they should not immediately be exposed to the fire, but restored to their usual tone and feeling, by immersing them in cold water, and afterwards applying warmth in the most careful and gradual manner. Persons subject to chopped hands in the winter time, should be careful to rub them quite dry after every washing; and to prevent their being injured by the weather, rub them with a mixture of fresh lard, honey, and the yolks of eggs; or a little goose fat will answer the purpose.

HARD DUMPLINGS. Make a paste of flour and water, with a little salt, and roll it into balls. Dust them with flour, and boil them nearly an hour. They are best boiled with a good piece of meat, and for variety, a few currants may be added.

HARES. If hung up in a dry cool place, they will keep a great time; and when imagined to be past eating, they are often in the highest perfection. They are never good if eaten when fresh killed. A hare will keep longer and eat better, if not opened for four or five days, or according to the state of the weather. If paunched when it comes from the field, it should be wiped quite dry, the heart and liver taken out, and the liver scalded to keep for stuffing.

Repeat this wiping every day, rub a mixture of pepper and ginger on the inside, and put a large piece of charcoal into it. If the spice be applied early, it will prevent that musty taste which long keeping in the damp occasions, and which also affects the stuffing. If an old hare is to be roasted, it should be kept as long as possible, and well soaked. This may be judged of, in the following manner. If the claws are blunt and rugged, the ears dry and tough, and the haunch thick, it is old. But if the claws are smooth and sharp, the ears easily tear, and the cleft in the lip is not much spread, it is young. If fresh and newly killed, the body will be stiff, and the flesh pale. To know a real leveret, it is necessary to look for a knob or small bone near the foot on its fore leg: if there be none, it is a hare.

HARE PIE. Cut up the hare, and season it; bake it with eggs and forcemeat, in a dish or raised crust. When cold take off the lid, and cover the meat with Savoury Jelly: see the article.

HARE SAUCE. This usually consists of currant jelly warmed up; or it may be made of half a pint of port, and a quarter of a pound of sugar, simmered together over a clear fire for about five minutes. It may also be made of half a pint of vinegar, and a quarter of a pound of sugar, reduced to a syrup.

HARE SOUP. Take an old hare unfit for other purposes, cut it into pieces, and put it into a jar; add a pound and a half of lean beef, two or three shank bones of mutton well cleaned, a slice of lean bacon or ham, an onion, and a bunch of sweet herbs. Pour on two quarts of boiling water, cover the jar close with bladder and paper, and set it in a kettle of water. Simmer till the hare is stewed to pieces, strain off the liquor, boil it up once, with a chopped anchovy, and add a spoonful of soy, a little cayenne, and salt. A few fine forcemeat balls, fried of a good brown, should be served in the tureen.

HARRICO OF MUTTON. Remove some of the fat, and cut the middle or best end of the neck into rather thin steaks. Flour and fry them in their own fat, of a fine light brown, but not enough for eating. Then put them into a dish while you fry the carrots, turnips, and onions; the carrots and turnips in dice, the onions sliced. They must only be warmed, and not browned. Then lay the steaks at the bottom of a stewpan, the vegetables over them, and pour on as much boiling water as will just cover them. Give them one boil, skim them well, and then set the pan on the side of the fire to simmer gently till all is tender. In three or four hours skim them; add pepper and salt, and a spoonful of ketchup.

HARRICO OF VEAL. Take the best end of a small neck, cut the bones short, but leave it whole. Then put it into a stewpan, just covered with brown gravy; and when it is nearly done, have ready a pint of boiled peas, six cucumbers pared and sliced, and two cabbage-lettuces cut into quarters, all stewed in a little good broth. Add them to the veal, and let them simmer ten minutes. When the veal is in the dish, pour the sauce and vegetables over it, and lay the lettuce with forcemeat balls round it.

HARTSHORN JELLY. Simmer eight ounces of hartshorn shavings with two quarts of water, till reduced to one. Strain and boil it with the rinds of four China oranges, and two lemons pared thin. When cool, add the juice of both, half a pound of sugar, and the whites of six eggs beaten to a froth. Let the jelly have three or four boils without stirring, and strain it through a jelly bag.

HASHED BEEF. Put into a stewpan, a pint and a half of broth or water, a large table-spoonful of mushroom ketchup, with the gravy saved from the beef. Add a quarter of an ounce of onion sliced very fine, and boil it about ten minutes. Put a large table-spoonful of flour into a basin, just wet it with a little water, mix it well together, then stir it into the broth, and boil it five or ten minutes. Rub it through a sieve, return it to the stewpan, put in the hash, and let it stand by the side of the fire till the meat is warm. A tea-spoonful of parsley chopped very fine, and put in five minutes before it is served up, will be an agreeable addition; or to give a higher relish, a glass of port wine, and a spoonful of currant jelly. Hashes and meats dressed a second time, should only simmer gently, till just warmed through.

HASHED DUCK. Cut a cold duck into joints, and warm it in gravy, without boiling, and add a glass of port wine.

HASHED HARE. Season the legs and wings first, and then broil them, which will greatly improve the flavour. Rub them with cold butter and serve them quite hot. The other parts, warmed with gravy, and a little stuffing, may be served separately.

HASHED MUTTON. Cut thin slices of dressed mutton, fat and lean, and flour them. Have ready a little onion boiled in two or three spoonfuls of water; add to it a little gravy, season the meat, and make it hot, but not to boil. Serve up the hash in a covered dish. Instead of onion, a clove, a spoonful of currant jelly, and half a glass of port wine, will give an agreeable venison flavour, if the meat be fine. For a change, the hash may be warmed up with pickled cucumber or walnut cut small.

HASHED VENISON. Warm it with its own gravy, or some of it without seasoning; but it should only be warmed through, and not boiled. If no fat be left, cut some slices of mutton fat, set it on the fire with a little port wine and sugar, and simmer it dry. Then put it to the hash, and it will eat as well as the fat of venison.

HASTY DISH OF EGGS. Beat up six eggs, pour them into a saucepan, hold it over the fire till they begin to thicken, and keep stirring from the bottom all the time. Then add a piece of butter the size of a walnut, stir it about till the eggs and water are thoroughly mixed, and the eggs quite dry. Put it on a plate, and serve it hot.

HASTY FRITTERS. Melt some butter in a saucepan, put in half a pint of good ale, and stir a little flour into it by degrees. Add a few currants, or chopped apples; beat them up quick, and drop a large spoonful at a time into the pan, till the bottom is nearly covered. Keep them separate, turn them with a slice; and when of a fine brown, serve them up hot, with grated sugar over them.

HASTY PUDDING. Boil some milk over a clear fire, and take it off. Keep putting in flour with one hand, and stirring it with the other, till it becomes quite thick. Boil it a few minutes, pour it into a dish, and garnish with pieces of butter. To make a better pudding, beat up an egg and flour into a stiff paste, and mince it fine. Put the mince into a quart of boiling milk, with a little butter and salt, cinnamon and sugar, and stir them carefully together. When sufficiently thickened, pour it into a dish, and stick bits of butter on the top. Or shred some suet, add grated bread, a few currants, the yolks of four eggs and the whites of two, with some grated lemon peel and ginger. Mix the whole together, and make it into balls the size and shape of an egg, with a little flour. Throw them into a skillet of boiling water, and boil them twenty minutes; but when sufficiently done, they will rise to the top. Serve with cold butter, or pudding sauce.

HATS. Gentlemen's hats are often damaged by a shower of rain, which takes off the gloss, and leaves them spotted. To prevent this, shake out the wet as much as possible, wipe the hat carefully with a clean handkerchief, observing to lay the beaver smooth. Then fix the hat in its original shape, and hang it to dry at a distance from the fire. Next morning, brush it several times with a soft brush in the proper direction, and the hat will have sustained but little injury. A flat iron moderately heated, and passed two or three times gently over the hat, will raise the gloss, and give the hat its former good appearance.

HAUNCH OF MUTTON. Keep it as long as it can be preserved sweet, and wash it with warm milk and water, or vinegar if necessary. When to be dressed especially, observe to wash it well, lest the outside should contract a bad flavour from keeping. Lay a paste of coarse flour on strong paper, and fold the haunch in it; set it a great distance from the fire, and allow proportionate time for the paste. Do not remove it till nearly forty minutes before serving, and then baste it continually. Bring the haunch nearer the fire before the paste is taken off, and froth it up the same as venison. A gravy must be made of a pound and a half of a loin of old mutton, simmered in a pint of water to half the quantity, and no seasoning but salt. Brown it with a little burnt sugar, and send it up in the dish. Care should be taken to retain a good deal of gravy in the meat, for though long at the fire, the distance and covering will prevent its roasting out. Serve with currant-jelly sauce.

HAUNCH OF VENISON. If it be the haunch of a buck, it will take full three hours and a half roasting; if a doe, about half an hour less. Venison should be rather under than overdone. Sprinkle some salt on a sheet of white paper, spread it over with butter, and cover the fat with it. Then lay a coarse paste on strong white paper, and cover the haunch; tie it with fine packthread, and set it at a distance from a good fire. Baste it often: ten minutes before serving take off the paste, draw the meat nearer the fire, and baste it with butter and a good deal of flour, to make it froth up well. Gravy for it should be put into a boat, and not into the dish, unless there is none in the venison. To make the gravy, cut off the fat from two or three pounds of a loin of old mutton, and set it in steaks on a gridiron for a few minutes just to brown one side. Put them into a saucepan with a quart of water, keep it closely covered for an hour, and simmer it gently. Then uncover it, stew it till the gravy is reduced to a pint, and season it with salt only. Currant-jelly sauce must be served in a boat. Beat up the jelly with a spoonful or two of port wine, and melt it over the fire. Where jelly runs short, a little more wine must be added, and a few lumps of sugar. Serve with French beans. If the old bread sauce be still preferred, grate some white bread, and boil it with port wine and water, and a large stick of cinnamon. When quite smooth, take out the cinnamon, and add some sugar.

HAY STACKS. In making stacks of new hay, care should be taken to prevent its heating and taking fire, by forming a tunnel completely through the centre. This may be done by stuffing a sack full of straw, and tying up the mouth with a cord; then make the rick round the sack, drawing it up as the rick advances, and taking it out when finished.

HEAD ACHE. This disorder generally arises from some internal cause, and is the symptom of a disease which requires first to be attended to; but where it is a local affection only, it may be relieved by bathing the part affected with spirits of hartshorn, or applying a poultice of elder flowers. In some cases the most obstinate pain is removed by the use of vervain, both internally in the form of a decoction, and also by suspending the herb round the neck. Persons afflicted with headache should beware of costiveness: their drink should be diluting, and their feet and legs kept warm. It is very obvious, that as many disorders arise from taking cold in the head, children should be inured to a light and loose covering in their infancy, by which means violent headaches might be prevented in mature age: and the maxim of keeping the feet warm and the head cool, should be strictly attended to.

HEAD AND PLUCK. Whether of lamb or mutton, wash the head clean, take the black part from the eyes, and the gall from the liver. Lay the head in warm water; boil the lights, heart, and part of the liver; chop them small, and add a little flour. Put it into a saucepan with some gravy, or a little of the liquor it was boiled in, a spoonful of ketchup, a small quantity of lemon juice, cream, pepper, and salt. Boil the head very white and tender, lay it in the middle of the dish, and the mince meat round it. Fry the other part of the liver with some small bits of bacon, lay them on the mince meat, boil the brains the same as for a calf's head, beat up an egg and mix with them, fry them in small cakes, and lay them on the rim of the dish. Garnish with lemon and parsley.

HEART BURN. Persons subject to this disorder, ought to drink no stale liquors, and to abstain from flatulent food. Take an infusion of bark, or any other stomachic bitter; or a tea-spoonful of the powder of gum arabic dissolved in a little water, or chew a few sweet almonds blanched. An infusion of anise seeds, or ginger, have sometimes produced the desired effect.

HEDGE HOG. Make a cake of any description, and bake it in a mould the shape of a hedge hog. Turn it out of the mould, and let it stand a day or two. Prick it with a fork, and let it remain all night in a dish full of sweet wine. Slit some blanched almonds, and stick about it, and pour boiled custard in the dish round it.

HERB PIE. Pick two handfuls of parsley from the stems, half the quantity of spinach, two lettuces, some mustard and cresses, a few leaves of borage, and white beet leaves. Wash and boil them a little, drain and press out the water, cut them small; mix a batter of flour, two eggs well beaten, a pint of cream, and half a pint of milk, and pour it on the herbs. Cover with a good crust, and bake it.

HERB TEA. If betony be gathered and dried before it begins to flower, it will be found to have the taste of tea, and all its good qualities, without any of its bad ones: it is also considered as a remedy for the headache. Hawthorn leaves dried, and one third of balm and sage, mixed together, will make a wholesome and strengthening drink. An infusion of ground ivy, mixed with a few flowers of lavender, and flavoured with a drop of lemon juice, will make an agreeable substitute for common tea. Various other vegetables might also be employed for this purpose; such as sage, balm, peppermint, and similar spicy plants; the flowers of the sweet woodroof, those of the burnet, or pimpernel rose; the leaves of peach and almond trees, the young and tender leaves of bilberry, and common raspberry; and the blossoms of the blackthorn, or sloe tree. Most of these when carefully gathered and dried in the shade, especially if they be managed like Indian tea-leaves, bear a great resemblance to the foreign teas, and are at the same time of superior flavour and salubrity.

HERBS FOR WINTER. Take any sort of sweet herbs, with three times the quantity of parsley, and dry them in the air, without exposing them to the sun. When quite dry, rub them through a hair sieve, put them in canisters or bottles, and keep them in a dry place: they will be useful for seasoning in the winter. Mint, sage, thyme, and such kind of herbs, may be tied in small bunches, and dried in the air: then put each sort separately into a bag, and hang it up in the kitchen. Parsley should be picked from the stalks as soon as gathered, and dried in the shade to preserve the colour. Cowslips and marigolds should be gathered dry, picked clean, dried in a cloth, and kept in paper bags.

HESSIAN SOUP. Clean the root of a neat's tongue very nicely, and half an ox's head, with salt and water, and soak them afterwards in water only. Then stew them in five or six quarts of water, till tolerably tender. Let the soup stand to be cold, take off the fat, which will do for basting, or to make good paste for hot meat pies. Put to the soup a pint of split peas, or a quart of whole ones, twelve carrots, six turnips, six potatoes, six large onions, a bunch of sweet herbs, and two heads of celery. Simmer them without the meat, till the vegetables are done enough to pulp with the peas through a sieve; and the soup will then be about the thickness of cream. Season it with pepper, salt, mace, allspice, a clove or two, and a little cayenne, all in fine powder. If the peas are bad, and the soup not thick enough, boil in it a slice of roll, and pass it through the cullender; or add a little rice flour, mixing it by degrees.—To make a ragout with the above, cut the nicest part of the head, the kernels, and part of the fat from the root of the tongue, into small thick pieces. Rub these with some of the above seasoning, putting them into a quart of the liquor reserved for that purpose before the vegetables were added; flour them well, and simmer till they are nicely tender. Then add a little mushroom and walnut ketchup, a little soy, a glass of port wine, and a tea-spoonful of made mustard, and boil all up together. Serve with small eggs and forcemeat balls. This furnishes an excellent soup and a ragout at a small expense.

HICCOUGH. A few small draughts of water in quick succession, or a tea-spoonful of vinegar, will often afford immediate relief. Peppermint water mixed with a few drops of vitriolic acid may be taken; and sometimes sneezing, or the stench of an extinguished tallow candle, has been found sufficient.

HIND QUARTER OF LAMB. Boil the leg in a floured cloth an hour and a quarter; cut the loin into chops, fry them, lay them round the leg, with a bit of parsley on each, and serve it up with spinach or brocoli.

HIND QUARTER OF PIG. To dress this joint lamb fashion, take off the skin, roast it, and serve it up with mint sauce. A leg of lamb stuffed like a leg of pork, and roasted, with drawn gravy, is very good. A loin of mutton also, stuffed like a hare, and basted with milk. Put gravy in the dish, served with currant jelly, or any other sauce.

HIVING OF BEES. When it is intended to introduce a swarm of bees into a new hive, it must be thoroughly cleaned, and the inside rubbed with virgin wax. A piece of nice honeycomb, made of very white wax, and about nine inches long, should be hung on the cross bars near the top of the hive, to form a kind of nest for the bees, and excite them to continue their work. The new hive being thus prepared, is then to be placed under an old one, before the bees begin to swarm, in such a manner as to be quite close, and to leave the bees no passage except into the new hive. As these insects generally work downwards, they will soon get into their new habitation; and when it is occupied by one half of the swarm, some holes must be made in the top of the old hive, and kept covered till the proper time of making use of them. Preparation being thus made, take the opportunity of a fine morning, about eight or nine o'clock, at which time most of the bees are out, gathering their harvest. The comb is to be cut through by means of a piece of iron wire, and the old hive separated from the new one. An assistant must immediately place the cover, which should be previously fitted, upon the top of the new one. The old hive is then to be taken to the distance of twenty or thirty yards, and placed firm upon a bench or table, but so as to leave a free space both above and below. The holes at the top being opened, one of the new boxes is to be placed on the top of the old hive, having the cover loosely fastened on it; and is to be done in such a manner, by closing the intervals between them with linen cloths, that the bees on going out by the holes on the top of the old hive can only go into the new one. But in order to drive the bees into the new hive, some live coals must be placed under the old one, upon which some linen may be thrown, to produce a volume of smoke; and the bees feeling the annoyance, will ascend to the top of the old hive, and at length will go through the holes into the new one. When they have nearly all entered, it is to be removed gently from the old hive, and placed under the box already mentioned, the top or cover having been taken off. If it should appear the next morning that the two boxes, of which the new hive is now composed, do not afford sufficient room for the bees, a third or fourth box may be added, under the others, as their work goes on, changing them from time to time so long as the season permits the bees to gather wax and honey. When a new swarm is to be hived, the boxes prepared as above and proportioned to the size of the swarm, are to be brought near the place where the bees have settled. The upper box with the cover upon it, must be taken from the others. The cross bars at the top should be smeared with honey and water, the doors must be closed, the box turned upside down, and held under the swarm, which is then to be shaken into it as into a common hive. When the whole swarm is in the box, it is to be carried to the other boxes, previously placed in their destined situation, and carefully put upon them. The interstices are to be closed with cement, and all the little doors closed, except the lowest, through which the bees are to pass. The hive should be shaded from the sun for a few days, that the bees may not be tempted to leave their new habitation. It is more advantageous however to form artificial swarms, than to collect those which abandon their native hives; and the hive here recommended is more particularly adapted to that purpose. By this mode of treatment, we not only avoid the inconveniences which attend the procuring of swarms in the common way, but obtain the advantage of having the hives always well stocked, which is of greater consequence than merely to increase their number; for it has been observed, that if a hive of four thousand bees give six pounds of honey, one of eight thousand will give twenty-four pounds. On this principle it is proper to unite two or more hives, when they happen to be thickly stocked. This may be done by scattering a few handfuls of balm in those hives which are to be united, which by giving them the same smell, they will be unable to distinguish one another. After this preparation, the hives are to be joined by placing them one upon the other, in the evening when they are at rest, and taking away those boxes which are nearly empty. All the little doors must be closed, except the lowest.——If bees are kept in single straw hives in the usual way, the manner of hiving them is somewhat different. They are first allowed to swarm, and having settled, they are then taken to the hive. If they fix on the lower branch of a tree, it may be cut off and laid on a cloth, and the hive placed over it, so as to leave room for the bees to ascend into it. If the queen can be found, and put into the hive, the rest will soon follow. But if it be difficult to reach them, let them remain where they have settled till the evening, when there will be less danger of escaping. After this the hive is to be placed in the apiary, cemented round the bottom, and covered from the wet at top. The usual method of uniting swarms, is by spreading a cloth at night upon the ground close to the hive, in which the hive with the new swarm is to be placed. By giving a smart stroke on the top of the hive, all the bees will drop into a cluster upon the cloth. Then take another hive from the beehouse, and place it over the bees, when they will ascend into it, and mix with those already there. Another way is to invert the hive in which the united swarms are to live, and strike the bees of the other hive into it as before. One of the queens is generally slain on this occasion, together with a considerable number of the working bees. To prevent this destruction, one of the queens should be sought for and taken, when the bees are beaten out of the hive upon the cloth, before the union is effected. Bees never swarm till the hive is too much crowded by the young brood, which happens in May or June, according to the warmth of the season. A good swarm should weigh five or six pounds; those that are under four pounds weight, should be strengthened by a small additional swarm. The size of the hive ought to be proportionate to the number of the bees, and should be rather too small than too large, as they require to be kept dry and warm in winter. In performing these several operations, it will be necessary to defend the hands and face from the sting of the bees. The best way of doing this is to cover the whole head and neck with a coarse cloth or canvas, which may be brought down and fastened round the waist. Through this cloth the motion of the bees may be observed, without fearing their stings; and the hands may be protected by a thick pair of gloves.

HODGE PODGE. Boil some slices of coarse beef in three quarts of water, and one of small beer. Skim it well, put in onions, carrots, turnips, celery, pepper and salt. When the meat is tender, take it out, strain off the soup, put a little butter and flour into the saucepan, and stir it well, to prevent burning. Take off the fat, put the soup into a stewpan, and stew the beef in it till it is quite tender. Serve up the soup with turnips and carrots, spinage or celery. A leg of beef cut in pieces, and stewed five or six hours, will make good soup; and any kind of roots or spices may be added or omitted at pleasure. Or stew some peas, lettuce, and onions, in a very little water, with a bone of beef or ham. While these are doing, season some mutton or lamb steaks, and fry them of a nice brown. Three quarters of an hour before serving, put the steaks into a stewpan, and the vegetables over them. Stew them, and serve all together in a tureen. Another way of making a good hodge podge, is to stew a knuckle of veal and a scrag of mutton, with some vegetables, adding a bit of butter rolled in flour.

HOG'S CHEEKS. If to be dried as usual, cut out the snout, remove the brains, and split the head, taking off the upper bone to make the chawl a good shape. Rub it well with salt, and next day take away the brine. On the following day cover the head with half an ounce of saltpetre, two ounces of bay salt, a little common salt, and four ounces of coarse sugar. Let the head be often turned, and after ten days smoke it for a week like bacon.

HOG'S EARS FORCED. Parboil two pair of ears, or take some that have been soused. Make a forcemeat of an anchovy, some sage and parsley, a quarter of a pound of chopped suet, bread crumbs, and only a little salt. Mix all these with the yolks of two eggs, raise the skin of the upper side of the ears, and stuff them with the mixture. Fry the ears in fresh butter, of a fine colour; then pour away the fat, and drain them. Prepare half a pint of rich gravy, with a glass of fine sherry, three tea-spoonfuls of made mustard, a little butter and flour, a small onion whole, and a little pepper or cayenne. Put this with the ears into a stewpan, and cover it close; stew it gently for half an hour, shaking the pan often. When done enough, take out the onion, place the ears carefully in a dish, and pour the sauce over them. If a larger dish is wanted, the meat from two feet may be added to the above.

HOG'S HEAD. To make some excellent meat of a hog's head, split it, take out the brains, cut off the ears, and sprinkle it with salt for a day. Then drain it, salt it again with common salt and saltpetre for three days, and afterwards lay the whole in a small quantity of water for two days. Wash it, and boil it till all the bones will come out. Skin the tongue, and take the skin carefully off the head, to put under and over. Chop the head as quick as possible, season it with pepper and salt, and a little mace or allspice berries.

Put the skin into a small pan, with the chopped head between, and press it down. When cold it will turn out, and make a kind of brawn. If too fat, a few bits of lean pork may be prepared in the same way, and added to it. Add salt and vinegar, and boil these with some of the liquor for a pickle to keep it.

HOG'S LARD. This should be carefully melted in a jar placed in a kettle of water, and boiled with a sprig of rosemary. After it has been prepared, run it into bladders that have been extremely well cleaned. The smaller they are, the better the lard will keep: if the air reaches it, it becomes rank. Lard being a most useful article for frying fish, it should be prepared with care. Mixed with butter, it makes fine crust.

HOLLOW BISCUITS. Mix a pound and a quarter of butter with three pounds and a half of flour, adding a pint of warm water. Cut out the paste with a wine glass, or a small tin, and set them in a brisk oven, after the white bread is drawn.

HONES. For joining them together, or cementing them to their frames, melt a little common glue without water, with half its weight of rosin, and a small quantity of red ochre.

HONEY. The honey produced by young bees, and which flows spontaneously, is purer than that expressed from the comb; and hence it is called virgin honey. The best sort is of a thick consistence, and of a whitish colour, inclining to yellow: it possesses an agreeable smell, and a pleasant taste. When the combs are removed from the hive, they are taken by the hand into a sieve, and left to drain into a vessel sufficiently wide for the purpose. After it has stood a proper time to settle, the pure honey is poured into earthen jars, tied down close to exclude the air.

HONEY VINEGAR. When honey is extracted from the combs, by means of pressure, take the whole mass, break and separate it, and into each tub or vessel put one part of combs, and two of water. Set them in the sun, or in a warm place, and cover them with cloths. Fermentation takes place in a few days, and continues from eight to twelve days, according to the temperature of the situation in which the operation is carried on. During the fermentation, stir the matter from time to time, and press it down with the hand, that it may be perfectly soaked. When the fermentation is over, put the matter to drain on sieves or strainers. At the bottom of the vessels will be found a yellow liquor, which must be thrown away, because it would soon contract a disagreeable smell, which it would communicate to the vinegar. Then wash the tubs, put into them the water separated from the other matter, and it will immediately begin to turn sour. The tubs must then be covered again with cloths, and kept moderately warm. A pellicle or skin is formed on the surface, beneath which the vinegar acquires strength. In a month's time it begins to be sharp, but must be suffered to stand a little longer, and then put into a cask, of which the bunghole is to be left open. It may then be used like any other vinegar. All kinds of vinegar may be strengthened by suffering it to be repeatedly frozen, and then separating the upper cake of ice or water from it.

HOOPING COUGH. This disorder generally attacks children, to whom it often proves fatal for want of proper management. Those who breathe an impure air, live upon poor sustenance, drink much warm tea, and do not take sufficient exercise, are most subject to this convulsive cough. In the beginning of the disorder, the child should be removed to a change of air, and the juice of onions or horseradish applied to the soles of the feet. The diet light and nourishing, and taken in small quantities; the drink must be lukewarm, consisting chiefly of toast and water, mixed with a little white wine. If the cough be attended with feverish symptoms, a gentle emetic must be taken, of camomile flowers, and afterwards the following liniment applied to the pit of the stomach. Dissolve one scruple of tartar emetic in two ounces of spring water, and add half an ounce of the tincture of cantharides: rub a tea-spoonful of it every hour on the lower region of the stomach with a warm piece of flannel, and let the wetted part be kept warm with flannel. This will be found to be the best remedy for the hooping cough.

HOPS. The quality of this article is generally determined by the price; yet hops may be strong, and not good. They should be bright, of a pleasant flavour, and have no foreign leaves or bits of branches among them. The hop is the husk or seed pod of the hop vine, as the cone is that of the fir tree; and the seeds themselves are deposited, like those of the fir, round a little soft stalk, enveloped by the several folds of this pod or cone. If in the gathering, leaves or tendrils of the vine are mixed with the hops, they may help to increase the weight, but will give a bad taste to the beer; and if they abound, they will spoil it. Great attention therefore must be paid to see that they are free from any foreign mixture. There are also numerous sorts of hops, varying in size, in form, and quality. Those that are best for brewing are generally known by the absence of a brown colour, which indicates perished hops; a colour between green and yellow, a great quantity of the yellow farina, seeds not too large or hard, a clamminess when rubbed between the fingers, and a lively pleasant smell, are the general indications of good hops. At almost any age they retain the power of preserving beer, but not of imparting a pleasant flavour; and therefore new hops are to be preferred. Supposing them to be of a good quality, a pound of hops may be allowed to a bushel of malt, when the beer is strong, or brewed in warm weather; but under other circumstances, half the quantity will be sufficient.

HOP-TOP SOUP. Take a quantity of hop-tops when they are in the greatest perfection, tie them in small bunches, soak them in water, and put them to some thin peas-soup. Boil them up, add three spoonfuls of onion juice, with salt and pepper. When done enough, serve them up in a tureen, with sippets of toasted bread at the bottom.

HORSERADISH POWDER. In November or December, slice some horseradish the thickness of a shilling, and lay it to dry very gradually in a Dutch oven, for a strong heat would very soon evaporate its flavour. When quite dry, pound it fine, and bottle it.

HORSERADISH VINEGAR. Pour a quart of the best vinegar on three ounces of scraped horseradish, an ounce of minced shalot, and a dram of cayenne. Let it stand a week, and it will give an excellent relish to cold beef, or other articles. A little black pepper and mustard, celery or cress seed, may be added to the above.

HOUSE DRAINS. The smell of house drains is oftentimes exceedingly offensive, but may be completely prevented by pouring down them a mixture of lime water, and the ley of wood ashes, or suds that have been used in washing. An article known by the name of a sink trap may be had at the ironmongers, which is a cheap and simple apparatus, for carrying off the waste water and other offensive matter from sinks and drains. But as the diffusion of any collection of filth tends to produce disease and mortality, it should not be suffered to settle and stagnate near our dwellings, and every possible care should be taken to render them sweet and wholesome.

HOUSE TAX. As the present system of taxation involves so important a part of the annual expenditure, and is in many instances attended with so much vexation and trouble, it concerns every housekeeper to be acquainted with the extent of his own liability, and of course to regulate his conveniences accordingly. It appears then, that every inhabited dwellinghouse, containing not more than six windows or lights, is subject to the yearly sum of six shillings and six-pence, if under the value of five pounds a year. But every dwellinghouse worth five pounds and under twenty pounds rent by the year, pays the yearly sum of one shilling and six-pence in the pound; every house worth twenty pounds and under forty pounds a year, two shillings and three-pence in the pound; and for every house worth forty pounds and upwards, the yearly sum of two shillings and ten-pence in the pound. These rents however are to be taken from the rates in which they are charged, and not from the rents which are actually paid.

HOUSEHOLD BREAD. Four ounces of salt are dissolved in three quarts of water, and mixed with a pint of yeast. This mixture is poured into a cavity made in a peck of second flour, placed in a large pan or trough. When properly kneaded and fermented, it is divided into pieces of a certain weight, and baked. Sometimes, in farm houses, a portion of rice flour, boiled potatoes, or rye meal, is mixed with the flour, previous to kneading the dough. The rye and rice serve to bind the bread, but the potatoes render it light and spongy.—Or, for a larger quantity, put a bushel of flour into a trough, two thirds wheat and one of rye. Mix a quart of yeast with nine quarts of warm water, and work it into the flour till it becomes tough. Leave it to rise about an hour; and as soon as it rises, add a pound of salt, and as much warm water as before. Work it well, and cover it with flannel. Make the loaves a quarter of an hour before the oven is ready; and if they weigh five pounds each, they will require to be baked two hours and a half.

HUNG BEEF. Make a strong brine with bay salt, common salt, and saltpetre, and put in ribs of beef for nine days. Then dry it, or smoke it in a chimney. Or rub the meat with salt and saltpetre, and repeat it for a fortnight, and dry it in wood smoke.

HUNGARY WATER. To one pint of highly rectified spirits of wine, put an ounce of the oil of rosemary, and two drams of the essence of ambergris. Shake the bottle well several times, and let the cork remain out twenty-four hours. Shake it daily for a whole month, and then put the water into small bottles for use.

HUNTER'S BEEF. To a round of beef that weighs twenty-five pounds, allow three ounces of saltpetre, three ounces of the coarsest sugar, an ounce of cloves, half an ounce of allspice, a nutmeg, and three handfuls of common salt, all in the finest powder. The beef should hang two or three days; then rub the above mixture well into it, and turn and rub it every day for two or three weeks. The bone must be taken out first. When to be dressed, dip it into cold water, to take off the loose spice; bind it up tight with tape, and put it into a pan with a tea-cupful of water at the bottom. Cover the top of the meat with shred suet, and the pan with a brown crust and paper, and bake it five or six hours. When cold, take off the paste and tape. The gravy is very fine, and a little of it is a great improvement to any kind of hash or soup. Both the gravy and the meat will keep some time. The meat should be cut with a very sharp knife, and quite smooth, to prevent waste.

HUNTER'S PUDDING. Mix together a pound of suet, a pound of flour, a pound of currants, and a pound of raisins stoned and cut. Add the rind of half a lemon finely shred, six peppercorns in fine powder, four eggs, a glass of brandy, a little salt, and as much milk as will make it of a proper consistence. Boil it in a floured cloth, or a melon mould, eight or nine hours. A spoonful of peach water may sometimes be added to change the flavour. This pudding will keep six months after it is boiled, if tied up in the same cloth when cold, and hung up, folded in writing paper to preserve it from the dust. When to be eaten, it must be boiled a full hour, and served with sweet sauce.

HYSTERICS. The sudden effusion of water on the face and hands, while the fit is on, and especially immersing the feet in cold water, will afford relief. Fetid smells are also proper; such as the burning of feathers, leather, or the smoke of sulphur, and the application of strong volatile alkali, or other pungent matters to the nostrils. To effect a radical cure, the cold bath, mineral waters, and other tonics are necessary. In Germany however, they cure hysteric affections by eating carraway seeds finely powdered, with a little ginger and salt, spread on bread and butter every morning.

I.

ICE FOR ICEING. To prepare artificial ice for articles of confectionary, procure a few pounds of real ice, reduce it nearly to powder, and throw a large handful or more of salt amongst it. This should be done in as cool a place as possible. The ice and salt being put into a pail, pour some cream into an ice pot, and cover it down. Then immerse it in the ice, and draw that round the pot, so as to enclose every part of it. In a few minutes stir it well with a spoon or spatula, removing to the centre those parts which have iced round the edges. If the ice cream or water be in a a form, shut the bottom close, and move the whole in the ice, as a spoon cannot be used for that purpose without danger of waste. There should be holes in the pail, to let off the ice as it thaws. When any fluid tends towards cold, moving it quickly will encrease that tendency; and likewise, when any fluid is tending to heat, stirring it will facilitate its boiling.

ICE CREAMS. Mix the juice of the fruits with as much sugar as will be wanted, before the cream is added, and let the cream be of a middling richness.

ICE WATERS. Rub some fine sugar on lemon or orange, to give the colour and flavour; then squeeze the juice of either on its respective peel. Add water and sugar to make a fine sherbet, and strain it before it be put into the ice-pot. If orange, the greater proportion should be of the china juice, and only a little of seville, and a small bit of the peel grated by the sugar. The juice of currants or raspberries, or any other sort of fruit, being squeezed out, sweetened, and mixed with water, may be prepared for iceing in the same way.

ICEING FOR CAKES. Beat and sift half a pound of fine sugar, put it into a mortar with four spoonfuls of rose water, and the whites of two eggs beaten and strained. Whisk it well, and when the cake is almost cold, dip a feather in the iceing, and cover the cake well. Set it in the oven to harden, but suffer it not to remain to be discoloured, and then keep it in a dry place. —For a very large cake, beat up the whites of twenty fresh eggs, and reduce to powder a pound of double refined sugar, sifted through a lawn sieve. Mix these well in a deep earthen pan, add orange flower water, barely sufficient to give it a flavour, and a piece of fresh lemon peel. Whisk it for three hours till the mixture is thick and white, then with a thin broad piece of board spread it all over the top and sides, and set it in a cool oven, and an hour will harden it.

ICEING FOR TARTS. Beat well together the yolk of an egg and some melted butter, smear the tarts with a feather, and sift sugar over them as they are put into the oven. Or beat up the white of an egg, wash the paste with it, and sift over some white sugar.

ILIAC PASSION. This dangerous malady, in which the motion of the bowels is totally impeded or inverted, arises from spasms, violent exertions of the body, eating of unripe fruit, drinking of sour liquors, worms, obstinate costiveness, and various other causes, which produce the most excruciating pain in the region of the abdomen. Large blisters applied to the most painful part, emollient clysters, fomentations, and the warm bath, are amongst the most likely means; but in many instances, this disorder is not to be controuled by medicine. No remedy however can be applied with greater safety or advantage, than frequent doses of castor oil: and if this fail, quicksilver in a natural state is the only medicine on which any reliance can be placed.

IMPERIAL. Put into a stone jar two ounces of cream of tartar, and the juice and paring of two lemons. Pour on them seven quarts of boiling water, stir it well, and cover it close. When cold, sweeten it with loaf sugar; strain, bottle, and cork it tight. This makes a very pleasant and wholesome liquor; but if drunk too freely, it becomes injurious. In bottling it off, add half a pint of rum to the whole quantity.

IMPERIAL CREAM. Boil a quart of cream with the thin rind of a lemon, and stir it till nearly cold. Have ready in a dish or bowl, in which it is to be served, the juice of three lemons strained, mixed with as much sugar as will sweeten the cream. Pour this into the dish from a large tea-pot, holding it high, and moving it about to mix with the juice. It should be made at least six hours before it is used; and if the day before, it would be still better.

IMPERIAL WATER. Put into an earthen pan, four ounces of sugar, and the rind of three lemons. Boil an ounce of cream of tartar in three quarts of water, and pour it on the sugar and lemon. Let it stand all night, clear it through a bag, and bottle it.

INCENSE. Compound in a marble mortar, a large quantity of lignum rhodium, and anise, with a little powder of dried orange peel, and gum benzoin. Add some gum dragon dissolved in rose water, and a little civet. Beat the whole together, form the mixture into small cakes, and place them on paper to dry. One of these cakes being burnt, will diffuse an agreeable odour throughout the largest apartment.

INDELIBLE INK. Gum arabic dissolved in water, and well mixed with fine ivory black, will make writing indelible. If the writing be afterwards varnished over with the white of an egg clarified, it will preserve it to any length of time.

INDIAN PICKLE. Lay a pound of white ginger in water one night; then scrape, slice, and lay it in salt in a pan, till the other ingredients are prepared. Peel and slice a pound of garlic, lay it in salt three days, and afterwards dry it in the sun. Salt and dry some long pepper in the same way: then prepare various sorts of vegetables in the following manner. Quarter some small white cabbages, salt them three days, then squeeze and lay them in the sun to dry. Cut some cauliflowers into branches, take off the green part of radishes, cut celery into lengths of about three inches, put in young French beans whole, and the shoots of elder, which will look like bamboo. Choose apples and cucumbers of a sort the least seedy, quarter them, or cut them in slices. All must be salted, drained, and dried in the sun, except the latter, over which some boiling vinegar must be poured. In twelve hours drain them, but use no salt. Put the spice into a large stone jar, adding the garlic, a quarter of a pound of mustard seed, an ounce of turmeric, and vinegar sufficient for the quantity of pickle. When the vegetables are dried and ready, the following directions must be observed. Put some of them into a half-gallon stone jar, and pour over them a quart of boiling vinegar. Next day take out those vegetables; and when drained, put them into a large stock jar. Boil the vinegar, pour it over some more of the vegetables, let them lie all night, and complete the operation as before. Thus proceed till each set is cleansed from the dust they may have contracted. Then to every gallon of vinegar, put two ounces of flour of mustard, gradually mixing in a little of it boiling hot, and stop the jar tight. The whole of the vinegar should be previously scalded, and set to cool before it is put to the spice. This pickle will not be ready for a year, but a small quantity may be got ready for eating in a fortnight, by only giving the cauliflower one scald in water, after salting and drying as above, but without the preparative vinegar: then pour the vinegar, which has the spice and garlic, boiling hot over it. If at any time it be found that the vegetables have not swelled properly, boiling the pickle, and pouring it hot over them, will make them plump.—Another way. Cut the heads of some good cauliflowers into pieces, and add some slices of the inside of the stalk. Put to them a white cabbage cut in pieces, with inside slices of carrot, turnips, and onions. Boil a strong brine of salt and water, simmer the vegetables in it one minute, drain them, and dry them on tins over an oven till they are shriveled up; then put them into a jar, and prepare the following pickle. To two quarts of good vinegar, put an ounce of the flour of mustard, one of ginger, one of long pepper, four of cloves, a few shalots, and a little horseradish. Boil the vinegar, put the vegetables into a jar, and pour it hot over them. When cold, tie them down, and add more vinegar afterwards, if necessary. In the course of a week or two, the pickle will be fit for use.

INDIGESTION. Persons of weak delicate habits, particularly the sedentary and studious, are frequently subject to indigestion. The liberal use of cold water alone, in drinking, washing, and bathing, is often sufficient to effect a cure. Drinking of sea water, gentle purgatives, with bark and bitters, light and nourishing food, early rising, and gentle exercise in the open air, are also of great importance.

INFECTION. During the prevalence of any infectious disease, every thing requires to be kept perfectly clean, and the sick room to be freely ventilated. The door or window should generally be open, the bed curtains only drawn to shade the light, clothes frequently changed and washed in cold water, all discharges from the patient instantly removed, and the floor near the bed rubbed every day with a wet cloth. Take also a hot brick, lay it in an earthen pan, and pour pickle vinegar upon it. This will refresh the patient, as well as purify the surrounding atmosphere. Those who are obliged to attend the patients, should not approach them fasting, nor inhale their breath; and while in their apartment, should avoid eating and drinking, and swallowing their own saliva. It will also be of considerable service to smell vinegar and camphor, to fumigate the room with tobacco, and to chew myrrh and cinnamon, which promote a plentiful discharge from the mouth. As soon as a person has returned from visiting an infected patient, he ought immediately to wash his mouth and hands with vinegar, to change his clothes, and expose them to the fresh air; and to drink an infusion of sage, or other aromatic herbs. After the disorder has subsided, the walls of the room should be washed with hot lime, which will render it perfectly sweet.

INFLAMMATIONS. In external inflammations, attended with heat and swelling of the part affected, cooling applications and a little opening medicine are the best adapted; and in some cases, cataplasms of warm emollient herbs may be used with advantage.

INFLAMMATION OF THE EYES. In this case leeches should be applied to the temples; and after the bleeding has ceased, a small blister may be tried, with a little opening medicine. Much benefit has been derived from shaving the head, cutting the hair, and bathing the feet in warm water. If the inflammation has arisen from particles of iron or steel falling into the eyes, the offending matter is best extracted by the application of the loadstone. If eyes are blood-shotten, the necessary rules are, an exclusion from light, cold fomentations, and abstinence from animal food and stimulating liquors. For a bruise in the eye, occasioned by any accident, the best remedy is a rotten apple, and some conserve of roses. Fold them in a piece of thin cambric, apply it to the part affected, and it will take out the bruise.

INFLAMMATION OF THE BOWELS. This is a complaint that requires great care. If the belly be swelled, and painful to the touch, apply flannels to it, dipped in hot water and wrung out, or use a warm bath. A blister should be employed as soon as possible, and mild emollient injections of gruel or barley water, till stools be obtained. The patient should be placed between blankets, and supplied with light gruel; and when the violence of the disorder is somewhat abated, the pain may be removed by opiate clysters. A common bread and milk poultice, applied as warm as possible to the part affected, has also been attended with great success: but as this disorder is very dangerous, it would be proper to call in medical assistance without delay.

INK. To make an excellent writing ink, take a pound of the best Aleppo galls, half a pound of copperas, a quarter of a pound of gum arabic, and a quarter of a pound of white sugar candy. Bruise the galls and beat the other ingredients fine, and infuse them together in three quarts of rain water. Let the mixture stand by the fire three or four days, and then boil it gently over a slow fire; or if infused in cold water, and afterwards well strained, it will nearly answer the same purpose. Care must be taken to obtain good materials, and to mix them in due proportion. To preserve the ink from mouldiness, it should be put into a large glass bottle with a ground stopper, and frequently shaked; but if a crust be formed, it should be carefully taken out, and not mixed with the ink. A little more gum and sugar candy may be added, to render the ink more black and glossy; but too much will make it sticky, and unfit for use.—Another method is to bruise a pound of good galls, black and heavy, and put them into a stone jar. Then pour on a gallon of rain water, nearly of a boiling heat, and let it stand by the fire about a fortnight. Afterwards add four ounces of green copperas or sulphate of iron, four ounces of logwood shavings, one ounce of alum, one of sugar candy, and four of gum arabic. Let the whole remain about two days longer in a moderate heat, stir the ingredients together once or twice a day, and keep the jar slightly covered. The ink is then to be strained through a flannel, put into a bottle with a little brandy at the top, well corked, and set by for use in a temperate place. A few cloves bruised with gum arabic, and put into the bottle, will prevent the ink from getting mouldy; and if some of superior quality be required, white wine or vinegar must be used instead of water.

INK POWDER. For the convenience of travellers by sea or by land, ink powders have been invented, which consist of nothing else than the substances employed in the composition of common ink, pounded and pulverized, so that it be instantaneously converted into ink by mixing it up with a little water. Walkden's ink powder is by far the best.

INK STAINS. The stains of ink, on cloth, paper, or wood, may be removed by almost all acids; but those acids are to be preferred, which are least likely to injure the texture of the stained substance. The muriatic acid, diluted with five or six times its weight of water, may be applied to the spot; and after a minute or two, may be washed off, repeating the application as often as it is found necessary. But the vegetable acids are attended with less risk, and are equally effectual. A solution of lemon or tartareous acid, in water, may be applied to the most delicate fabrics, without any danger of injuring them: and the same solution will discharge writing, but not printing ink. Hence they may be employed in cleaning books which have been defaced by writing on the margin, without impairing the text. Lemon juice and the juice of sorrel will also remove ink stains, but not so easily as the concrete acid of lemons, or citric acid. On some occasions it will be found sufficient, only to dip the spotted part in the fine melted tallow of a mould candle, and afterwards wash it in the usual way.

INSECTS. The most effectual remedy against the whole tribe of insects, which prey upon plants and vegetables, is the frequent use of sulphur, which should be dusted upon the leaves through a muslin rag or dredging box, or fumed on a chaffing dish of burning charcoal. This application will also improve the healthiness of plants, as well as destroy their numerous enemies. Another way is to boil together an equal quantity of rue, wormwood, and tobacco, in common water, so as to make the liquor strong, and then to sprinkle it on the leaves every morning and evening. By pouring boiling water on some tobacco and the tender shoots of elder, a strong decoction may also be made for this purpose, and shed upon fruit trees with a brush: the quantity, about an ounce of tobacco and two handfuls of elder to a gallon of water. Elder water sprinkled on honeysuckles and roses, will prevent insects from lodging on them. If a quantity of wool happen to be infected with insects, it may be cleansed in the following manner. Dissolve a pound of alum, and as much cream of tartar, in a quart of boiling water, and add two full gallons of cold water to it. The wool is then to be soaked in it for several days, and afterwards to be washed and dried.

INSIDE OF A SIRLOIN. Cut out all the meat and a little fat, of the inside of a cold sirloin of beef, and divide it into pieces of a finger's size and length. Dredge the meat with flour, and fry it in butter, of a nice brown. Drain the butter from the meat, and toss it up in a rich gravy, seasoned with pepper, salt, anchovy, and shalot. It must not be suffered to boil; and before serving, add two spoonfuls of vinegar. Garnish with crimped parsley.

INVISIBLE INK. Boil half an ounce of gold litharge well pounded, with a little vinegar in a brass vessel for half an hour. Filter the liquid through paper, and preserve it in a bottle closely corked. This ink is to be used with a clean pen, and the writing when dry will become invisible. But if at any time it be washed over with the following mixture, it will instantly become black and legible. Put some quicklime and red orpiment in water, place some warm ashes under it for a whole day, filter the liquor, and cork it down. Whenever applied in the slightest degree, it will render the writing visible.

IRISH BEEF. To twenty pounds of beef, put one ounce of allspice, a quarter of an ounce of mace, cinnamon, and nutmeg, and half an ounce each of pepper and saltpetre. Mix all together, and add some common salt. Put the meat into a salting pan, turn it every day, and rub it with the seasoning. After a month take out the bone, and boil the meat in the liquor it was pickled in, with a proper quantity of water. It may be stuffed with herbs, and eaten cold.

IRISH PANCAKES. Beat eight yolks and four whites of eggs, strain them into a pint of cream, sweeten with sugar, and add a grated nutmeg. Stir three ounces of butter over the fire, and as it melts pour it to the cream, which should be warm when the eggs are put to it. Mix it smooth with nearly half a pint of flour, and fry the pancakes very thin; the first with a bit of butter, but not the others. Serve up several at a time, one upon another.

IRISH STEW. Take five thick mutton chops, or two pounds off the neck or loin; four pounds of potatoes, peeled and divided; and half a pound of onions, peeled and sliced. Put a layer of potatoes at the bottom of a stewpan, then a couple of chops, and some of the onions, and so on till the pan is quite full. Add a small spoonful of white pepper, about one and a half of salt, and three quarters of a pint of broth or gravy. Cover all close down, so as to prevent the escape of steam, and let them stew two hours on a very slow fire. It must not be suffered to burn, nor be done too fast: a small slice of ham will be an agreeable addition.

IRON MOULDS. Wet the injured part, rub on a little of the essential salt of lemons, and lay it on a hot waterplate. If the linen becomes dry, wet it and renew the process, observing that the plate is kept boiling hot. Much of the powder sold under the name of salt of lemons is a spurious preparation, and therefore it is necessary to dip the linen in a good deal of water, and to wash it as soon as the stain is removed, in order to prevent the part from being worn into holes by the acid.

IRON POTS. To cure cracks or fissures in iron pots or pans, mix some finely sifted lime with whites of eggs well beaten, till reduced to a paste. Add some iron file dust, and apply the composition to the injured part, and it will soon become hard and fit for use.

IRON AND STEEL. Various kinds of polished articles, in iron and steel, are in danger of being rusted and spoiled, by an exposure to air and moisture. A mixture of nearly equal quantities of fat, oil varnish, and the rectified spirits of turpentine, applied with a sponge, will give a varnish to those articles, which prevents their contracting any spots of rust, and preserves their brilliancy, even though exposed to air and water. Common articles of steel or iron may be preserved from injury by a composition of one pound of fresh lard, an ounce of camphor, two drams of black lead powder, and two drams of dragon's blood in fine powder, melted over a slow fire, and rubbed on with a brush or sponge, after it has been left to cool.

ISINGLASS JELLY. Boil an ounce of isinglass in a quart of water, with a few cloves, lemon peel, or wine, till it is reduced to half the quantity. Then strain it, and add a little sugar and lemon juice.

ISSUE OINTMENT. For dressing blisters, in order to keep them open, make an ointment of half an ounce of Spanish flies finely powdered, mixed with six ounces of yellow basilicon ointment.

ITALIAN BEEF STEAKS. Cut a fine large steak from a rump that has been well kept, or from any tender part. Beat it, and season with pepper, salt, and onion. Lay it in an iron stewpan that has a cover to fit it quite close, and set it by the side of the fire without water. It must have a strong heat, but care must be taken that it does not burn: in two or three hours it will be quite tender, and then serve with its own gravy.

ITCH. Rub the parts affected with the ointment of sulphur, and keep the body gently open by taking every day a small dose of sulphur and treacle. When the cure is effected, let the clothes be carefully fumigated with sulphur, or the contagion will again be communicated. The dry itch requires a vegetable diet, and the liberal use of anti-scorbutics: the parts affected may be rubbed with a strong decoction of tobacco.

IVORY. Bones and ivory may be turned to almost any use, by being softened in the following manner. Boil some sage in strong vinegar, strain the liquor through a piece of cloth, and put in the articles. In proportion to the time they are steeped in the liquor, ivory or bones will be capable of receiving any new impression.